LIVERPOOL ON THE BRINK

LIVERPOOL ON THE BRINK

One city's struggle against Government cuts

Michael Parkinson

POLICY JOURNALS

To Joey – 'forever young'

Published and distributed by

POLICY JOURNALS

The Old Vicarage
Marlston Road
Hermitage
Berks RG16 9SU

ISBN 0 946967 06 7 (hardback)
ISBN 0 946967 07 5 (paperback)

Designed by David Cutting Graphics
Printed by the Burlington Press, Cambridge

CONTENTS

ACKNOWLEDGMENTS

This book tries to discuss in a serious but accessible way, political responses in Liverpool to the city's financial and economic decline. It was difficult to write for several reasons. The story had no obvious beginning, middle or end. Its subject was a moving target. Trying to interpret events as they took place was emotionally draining for someone who lives in, works in and cares for Liverpool. Also local government finance and budgets are very confusing and I needed enormous help from several people even to make sense of the material I have used. I received an extraordinary degree of cooperation from nearly everyone most intimately involved in Liverpool's financial decision-making during the past two years. However, given the controversial nature of those decisions, many of those people will disagree with much I have written. But I have tried to be honest as well as present Liverpool's case fairly.

In many respects, I regard this book as a collective effort and should like to thank the following people who, in different ways, helped me understand the present conflict and where it fits into the complexities of Liverpool's politics: Paul Astbury, Gideon Ben-Tovim , Marge Ben-Tovim, Mike Black, Graham Burgess, Tony Byrne, David Copley, Peter Cresswell, Peter Dowd, John Farrell, Peter Ferguson, Colin Forrester, Derek Hatton, John Hamilton, John Kenny, Tony Lane, Ian Lowes, Paul Luske, Steve McGriskin, Alan Maher, John Nelson, Roger O'Hara, Andy Pink, Jimmy Rand, Michael Reddington, Vicki Roberts, Dave Robertson, Tony Schorah, Harry Smith, Eric Sorenson, Alfred Stocks, Cyril Taylor, Ian Williams and Chris Williamson. Catherine Meredith first made me appreciate the crucial importance of housing in Liverpool's politics. Geoff Walsh sparked my interest in the subject and led me through ten years of budget records with patience and great good humour. Steve Ferguson read the manuscript and encouraged me especially at an early stage. Professor Mik Laver shared responsibility for the survey of Liverpool voters. My colleagues in the department of politics at Liverpool University provided a supportive intellectual environment for my work. A number of people who in some ways contributed most to this book have asked not to be named.

My research on Liverpool politics was originally supported by a grant from the Social Science Research Council. I doubt if this is the book they had in mind. But I shall always be grateful to Professor Mike Goldsmith for his support at that time. Equally, Stephen Wilks showed great tolerance and understanding throughout. Professor Jane Marceau gave me the confidence to start the project. Pat Brooksbank, who struggled with my appalling handwriting and endless revisions, made it possible to complete it. The Reverend Peter Brain was a constant supporter, who read and commented thoughtfully on every page of the text. If the moral dimension is not evident enough in the book, I apologise to him. Two other people need special mention. They both sensed I had something to say about an important issue and encouraged me to say it. John Gretton was the best possible editor, providing an incisive blend of intellectual support and criticism precisely when each was required. Any merit this book may have is due in large part to him. My primary debt is to a senior colleague at Liverpool University, Professor David Jennings. He took a reassuring interest in my work and provided the continuing moral and financial support, without which this book would never even have been written. I hope it repays his trust.

Finally, only those who know Fran realise how much she has contributed by just being there. And Jessica always said you could only do your best work, and then hope.

Michael Parkinson
Centre for Urban Studies,
Liverpool University.
October, 1985.

THE ORIGINS OF THE BUDGET CRISIS – 1974-1983

1

Cities are the creatures of economics. They survive as communities if they can cope with the vagaries of economic change. Once economic decline sets in, every aspect of their life is threatened. Liverpool is the perfect illustration of that process, for decline has eaten into the city's economy, society and politics. The story began with the port. It made the city great and in the 19th century gave it more millionaires than any other provincial city in Britain. But the port's decline left Liverpool with a legacy that now makes economic survival, let alone recovery, problematic at best. Its fall began with the impact of the 1930s depression upon world trade. But since 1945, changes in the national and international economy have dramatically speeded up the process. And the city has never really recovered its balance.

For a brief period during the 1960s, government policies to strengthen its economy promised to arrest the process. But it proved to be a false dawn. Since then, decline has turned into collapse and Liverpool threatens to become the first deindustrialised city in the nation. In the 1980s, the city is economically marooned: it is in the wrong place, based on the wrong kind of economic activity with an outdated infrastructure and an underqualified labour force. It is increasingly a 'branch plant economy' which has become peripheral to the mainstream international capitalist economy. And economic failure has produced a range of social problems in the city as intense and intractable as any in Western Europe. In 1981 tear gas had to be used by police for the first time on the British mainland to put down 'a poor people's revolt' in its inner city.

Until quite recently, the city's economic misfortunes did not have a major direct impact upon the health of the municipal economy itself, because high levels of public expenditure and a relatively generous government grant system protected the local authority from the most severe financial effects of structural decline. Economic privation was experienced primarily by vulnerable individuals and groups in the community. But cuts in central government support since the mid-1970s, but especially under the Conservatives in the 1980s, have changed that. The decline in local economic resources has become a much more serious problem for the city because they now have to make a larger contribution to the local authority's income to compensate for the drop in national support. When the Conservatives took power in 1979 central government was providing 62 per cent of the city's net income and the rates over 37 per cent. By 1983 the Government's contribution had dropped to 44 per cent and the rates had risen to over 55 per cent. By the mid-1980s cuts in government financial support had turned economic failure into fiscal crisis and brought Liverpool to the edge of municipal bankruptcy. And this all spilt over into the city's political life as a Militant-led Labour party used its budget crisis to challenge the authority of a free market Conservative Government. Liverpool now stands at the centre of the economic, social and ideological forces facing British cities. It is a test case of how the country responds politically to long-term urban decline.

From economic collapse to financial crisis

The port dominated Liverpool's economy after the first dock was built in the early part of the 18th century. But in the second half of the century, trade exploded. The slave trade played a major part in the boom – by the end of the century Liverpool supplied three quarters of the country's slaving ships, which in peak years carried 50,000 slaves. But human beings were not the only goods in which Liverpool traded as it became a vast importer of raw materials as well as a major exporter. Throughout the 19th century Liverpool flourished even further. Trade trebled between 1830 and 1860 and again between 1860 and the outbreak of the first world war. By 1914, the port was second only to London, with one third of all British exports and one quarter of all imports going through Liverpool.

The port also dominated the labour market, with some serious long-term consequences. Outside the commercial sector, jobs were mainly semi- and unskilled, casual, irregular and poorly paid. Unlike other cities, a core of skilled workers did not develop, because manufacturing never took off in Liverpool. This overdependence on the port, and the relative absence of an industrial base, always worried the city's leaders. But the unbalanced character of its economy did not seem important until the collapse of the international economy and the depression after the first world war. Liverpool has been in decline ever since as nothing else has replaced the port. By the early 1930s unemployment in Liverpool reached a peak of 28 per cent and throughout the decade was always at least one and a half times the national average. In the late 1940s unemployment actually rose to two and a half times the national average. Government policies in the 1950s did bring some new manufacturing jobs to the Merseyside area, but other factory closures and the continuing loss of jobs in the port cancelled them out. And the city's unfavourable industrial structure remained unchanged.

The 1960s initially promised better things for Liverpool as government policy to redistribute industry appeared to break the pattern of long-term decline. The sticks and carrots of regional policy led to the important, if reluctant, establishment of a branch of the British car industry on Merseyside, with an investment programme of £m65 which created 25,000 jobs. For the first time in its history, in the early 1960s manufacturing became a growth sector in Merseyside. And by the end of the decade, despite some reservations, there was a feeling that the place was on the road to recovery. But the brief flirtation with manufacturing did not continue and the gains of the 1960s were not sustained. Between 1966 and 1977 350 plants closed or transferred production elsewhere with the loss of 40,000 jobs. At the same time the port continued its decline. Its share of total imports and exports was almost halved from 15 to 8 per cent, and the workforce reduced to 3,000 from 25,000 in 1945. Again between 1966 and 1976, employment in Merseyside fell by 14 per cent, much more than either the national or regional average. By the late 1970s, Liverpool's manufacturing economy seemed on the verge of collapse.

The crucial problem of Liverpool's manufacturing economy is the pattern of ownership. Far more than in other cities, its manufacturing is dominated by a small number of very large absentee employers. At the beginning of the 1980s, for example, 57 per cent of manufacturing jobs were in plants employing over 1,000 workers. By contrast the national figure was only 29 per cent. In 1979, less than 1 per cent of the city's firms provided nearly 40 per cent of total employment. By 1985, seven large firms controlled almost half of all the 47,000 manufacturing jobs in the city. And between 1981 and 1985 these seven firms had shed 30 per cent of their jobs.

With few exceptions, these very large firms which were frequently although not always established as a result of regional policy during the 1950s and 1960s, are externally, not locally, controlled. And this dependence upon externally controlled firms is increasing. In 1965, 51 per cent of Liverpool's manufacturing firms were non-locally controlled. By 1975 this had risen to 70 per cent. In the 1980s only one of the twenty largest manufacturing companies on Merseyside is actually locally controlled. The problem is that such firms tend to be branch plants of national or multi-national corporations who make investment and disinvestment decisions in terms of national and international, not local, markets. They have no particular commitment to the people or the place of Liverpool. Their plants are particularly vulnerable to the loss of jobs as these companies rationalise and restructure production during a recession. Production in Liverpool tends to be cut back first. And when factories do close the job losses inevitably wipe out any marginal – and often painfully achieved – gains, by the small firm sector of the economy. Between 1979 and 1984 almost half its manufacturing jobs, 40,000, were lost in this way as Liverpool became known as the Bermuda Triangle of British capitalism. In the mid 1980s, the city had lost control of its economic destiny.

The decline of manufacturing has been aggravated by the failure of the service sector to bring new growth to Liverpool, in contrast to other places. Although services not manufacturing have traditionally dominated Liverpool's economy, the bulk of those jobs have been in the 'blue-collar' sector – nationalised industries, transport, retailing and distribution. Liverpool did not develop a significant white-collar service sector. And even though the sector did grow in the 1970s it lagged behind the national trends. Most important, jobs in the prestigious and growing insurance, banking, finance, business, professional and scientific services, actually declined in Liverpool, while they grew nationally. The only white collar growth that did take place in the 1970s was in the public sector – in central government, local authorities, the health service. And by 1981 even this sector was already in decline from the peak year of 1977 as public expenditure cuts had begun to have their impact. Between 1976 and 1979, for example, the number of Liverpool city council jobs fell by 7 per cent.

From 1971 to 1985 total employment in the city fell by 33 per cent in contrast to the national figure of only 3 per cent. And this brought heavy rates of unemployment. In fact, Merseyside has had the highest rate of unemployment of any English conurbation in every decade since the 1950s. But the position worsened considerably during the 1970s as the rate of unemployment in Liverpool quadrupled from 5 per cent to 20 per cent. By 1985 it was 27 per cent, double the national average.

Unemployment also lasts longer in Liverpool than elsewhere. In 1979, 37 per cent of registered unemployed people in Liverpool had been out of work for more than a year compared with only 24 per cent nationally. By 1985 the national figure was 39 per cent, but Liverpool's was 53 per cent. This is crucial since after one year, people go off unemployment benefit on to social security and the money they get and can spend drops significantly, depressing the local economy further. Although national figures show the same underlying trend in the 1980s, Liverpool's economic problems are still more serious than any other city's. The Parliamentary select committee on the environment said so in 1983. And this Conservative Government has admitted it as well. The Director of the Government's special Merseyside Task Force, Eric Sorenson, was asked by that select committee why so much attention had been paid to Liverpool's problems in recent years. He replied simply 'Because they are worse.'

This is why public sector employment has become so crucial in Liverpool. In the late 1970s, close to 70 per cent of all jobs in the city were in the service sector. About half of them were actually public sector jobs. The city council itself accounted for one third of all public sector jobs. By 1985, decline in other parts of the public sector meant that the council employed almost 40 per cent of people in public sector jobs, making it even more important as an employer in the city. Because of the peculiar structure of its economy, Liverpool depends more on public spending for jobs than other cities. This has dramatically affected its politics. Arguments about cuts in public spending and job losses dominated local political debate in the past decade, and became central to the conflict between the city and the Government in the 1980s. The Conservative Government's view was that public employment increased taxes which drove out the private sector. The Labour party argued that the private sector had abandoned the city anyway, and that public employment was not part of the problem, but part of the solution to it.

In 1984, the Labour council seized upon the scale of economic decline and the very high levels of unemployment in the city, to mount an ideological attack upon the Conservative Government's policies for Liverpool. It argued that its cuts in spending were threatening the city's remaining jobs, by depressing one of the few viable parts of the local economy, the public sector. But it did not need a political party to make these arguments. They had been very well known for a very long time. The significance of these economic trends, and their dangers for the city, had been pointed out several years before Labour took control of the council, by the city's chief planning officer. His 1981 report entitled Local Economic Trends And Future Prospects, emphasised that the consequences of economic decline and unemployment had extended far beyond the individuals, families and communities into the municipal economy itself. It had set in motion a cycle of decline which included increases in vacant and derelict land and buildings; a continuing loss of population; declining levels of personal income and expenditure; a loss of revenue to the local authority; a loss of taxation and an increase in social security expenditure.

His report estimated that between 1974 and 1979, at a time when the city's economic problems were worsening, and the need for public sector action to ameliorate their effects had risen, the level of the city's economic activity in real money terms had declined. As for the city council, total income fell by 18 per cent; rate income fell by 25 per cent; and total real net expenditure fell by 14 per cent from its peak level of 1975/76. This in turn had affected the local economy, by reducing demand for locally-produced goods and services. On top of that the city council was faced with the prospect of substantial rate rises if it wanted to maintain existing expenditure and income levels, as the Government reduced financial support to it through the grant system. In other words, the city's economic failure had been turned into serious financial strain for the local authority. And the social and political consequences were likely to be bleak. In the planning officer's view, the extreme variations within the city itself – of unemployment rates, job prospects and income levels – would only have 'a detrimental and lasting effect on its social and economic fabric.' That is, as it entered the 1980s, the city was in danger of becoming socially and economically polarised, with quite unpredictable consequences.

Urban protest and Government responses

That report proved prophetic. Several months later, in July 1981, a furious bout of rioting, looting and arson broke out in the inner city area of Toxteth, the home of some of the poorest black and white people in the city. At the end of two weeks sporadic violence, a young man was dead, hundreds of police and unknown numbers of civilians had been injured, and £m11 of damage had been unleashed upon the neighbourhood's public buildings, homes and shops. Police were drafted in from many parts of the country and tear gas was used to control some of the worst pitched battles between hundreds of residents and the police. Initially the riots had been sparked off by an incident in which police attempted to arrest a local black youth. This set alight simmering resentments and conflicts between the local black community and police. And it opened up much larger questions about race relations in the city, and the serious degree of unacknowledged racism in Liverpool that in fact none of the political parties has ever admitted or dealt with. But the insurrection also spread to local whites, as the dispossessed of the inner city rose into 'a poor people's revolt' against authority. And a Government had been frightened.

As Michael Heseltine's 'secret' 'It took a riot' memo to the Cabinet pointed out, the Government only began to take seriously the problems of economic and social deprivation in the poorest city in Britain, when they threatened public order. And after the tear gas had dispersed the rioters and the smoke had settled, a bevy of senior Ministers toured the riot zone to witness the extent of the damage, and search for a credible Government response to the 'Liverpool problem.' It came up with a new initiative, a special Minister for Merseyside, Michael Heseltine, supported by a new administrative unit, the Merseyside Task Force, consisting of civil servants from three government Departments and secondees from the much vaunted private sector. The new team was supposed to devise innovative strategies and projects which would make an impact upon Liverpool's long-term problems, especially unemployment and housing. But four years later in 1985, their failure to change the dimensions of those problems had left the public sceptical of, and the local authority more hostile to, Government attempts to help the city.

The fact is that, despite the novelty of the administrative arrangements, Task Force stood firmly in a well-established tradition of 'special' government initiatives for inner Liverpool during the past twenty years. Since the 1960s, the city has been the recipient, or victim, of every urban experiment invented, including Tony Crosland's educational priority areas, Jim Callaghan's traditional urban programme, Roy Jenkin's community development projects, the Home Office's Brunswick neighbourhood project, Peter Walker's inner area studies, Peter Shore's inner city partnerships, Geoffrey Howe's enterprise zones and Michael Heseltine's urban development corporations. Two decades' experience of those policies had not substantially improved the city's problems. But it had fundamentally coloured local people's perceptions, and made them intensely sceptical of what would be done for Liverpool through 'special initiatives'.

The initiatives failed for a variety of familiar reasons. Partly it was a problem of analysis and definition. Many of the earlier ones especially focused on the social symptoms of Liverpool's decline, but failed to identify or deal with the underlying structural problem, the economic decline of the city. Partly it was a question of resources. The amount of money involved was relatively trivial in relation either to the scale of the problems or even to the resources that go into conventional government programmes. Also they tended to be ad hoc experiments, which concentrated on specific problems or too narrowly defined areas or communities in the city. And they often remained divorced from mainstream government programmes, such as industrial, regional or housing policy, which pulled in different directions from inner city initiatives. They rarely succeeded in getting all the government Departments which had an impact upon the inner city to play a part, and as a result the policies frequently lacked coherence.

But more than that, the experience of such initiatives led many local politicians and officials to conclude that central government was not seriously committed to trying to solve the city's problems. In part this was because the inner city went up and down on the national political agenda, not primarily in relation to real need but rather to narrow political opportunism, such as recapturing the inner city Labour vote or keeping the lid on social protest. Programmes often stopped just as they got going. Or the direction changed part way through the policy, often when the government itself changed hands. Local politicians and officials frequently felt that central government imposed the policies upon them without consulting them but expected them to make them work anyway. Most of these criticisms would apply to Labour Governments. But they pale into insignificance in comparison with local criticism levied at the central government since the Conservatives took control. With Labour Governments, Liverpool's politicians and officials felt that the urban programme, if ineffectual, was at least benign in intent. But under the Conservatives, the feeling in Liverpool has grown that policy is malign. Partly it is because Government money has been moving away from the authority, even if the special initiatives and the urban programme resources themselves have actually gone up. The Government has taken away more with one hand than it has given back with the other. Partly it is the ideological thrust of urban policy under the Conservatives, which replaces public sector spending with private-sector led urban regeneration.

But most importantly it is the pervasive feeling among many local politicians that Liverpool has no place in the Conservatives' scheme of things, who simply do not care about its people or its problems. In local eyes, Liverpool is redundant, economically and politically, to the Conservatives. And there are certainly very few Conservative votes left in Liverpool. As the Conservative party has flourished in the country at large, Liverpool has rejected it, getting rid of every MP and leaving just a dozen or so councillors. For whatever reason, relations between Liverpool and the Government were slowly worsening during the 1970s, as the city's economic decline continued and national responses were unable to cope with it. The place clearly needed help but felt Government was not prepared to give it. And this increased political distrust.

By the early 1980s the Conservative Government reciprocated these feelings. It regarded the city as expensive, inefficient and badly run – incapable of responding adequately, politically or administratively, to the scale of the problems it faced. Even though it can be argued that central government was equally responsible for recent failures of urban policy, the Government thought Liverpool missed the opportunity it was given to help itself, classically blaming the victims for their misfortunes. But most crucially, by the mid 1980s the Conservatives saw Liverpool as the power base of the Militant Tendency. And they wanted to defeat it. The scene was set for a political confrontation.

Parties and politics in Liverpool

The peculiarities of Liverpool politics during the past decade directly contributed to rising tensions between the city and Government. For specific historical reasons, party politics in Liverpool are unlike those in any other city. The casual and relatively unskilled nature of the workforce with its absence of skilled craft unions, compounded by religious conflicts between the immigrant Irish Catholic and working class Protestant communities, meant that the Labour party took a very long time to establish its natural electoral majority in the most proletarian of English cities. The divisions within the working class vote, and the strength of Protestantism, prevented Labour taking power in Liverpool until 1955, thirty years after many other northern industrial towns had been captured. And between the mid-1950s and early 1970s, Labour had to share control of the city with the Conservatives.

The importance of Catholicism meant Labour always had a very powerful right-wing presence, which guaranteed continuing ideological conflict within the party. It also contributed to a politics of personality, patronage, corruption and bossism in the Liverpool Labour party which reached its acme under the Braddocks who ran the city in the 1950s and early 1960s, and has never been completely eliminated. Labour has also had a long tradition of appointing right-wing MPs who spent much of their career locked in conflict with their more left-wing constituency parties. Indeed in the late 1970s three of them defected to the Social Democratic Party either before or after being deselected. The classic case was Sir Arthur Irvine, the right-wing absentee MP for Edgehill, who had been Solicitor-General in Wilson's Cabinet and survived many attempted coups before finally dying in office. But his inadequate tenure of office had laid the ground for the Liberals and David Alton to take over the constituency.

The combination of these factors meant that Labour's electoral grip of the city was always tenuous and vulnerable in the 1960s and 1970s. But it was broken in the early 1970s by an extraordinary phenomenon which has never been repeated in any other large English city – the emergence of a Liberal party which took seats and votes from both major parties and controlled the city for most of a decade. In the late 1960s and early 1970s, the Liberal party had barely any organisation, supporters or councillors. But in 1973, elections were held for the new Liverpool district council which was to come into office in 1974, and the Liberals scored a shattering victory, taking many former seats from Labour and decimating the Conservatives. With this began the most unusual decade of municipal politics in Liverpool. Between 1973 and 1983 no party had an overall majority, there were constant hung councils, minority and coalition administrations and confusion. The resulting failure of any administration to deal with many of the city's most pressing issues during this period contributed directly to the current crisis as the city's services, in many respects became inefficient and expensive.

The extraordinary success of the Liberals in the 1970s rested partly on their own virtues, but also on their opponents' vices. The Labour party in particular was beset with problems. Its greatest millstone was that during the 1960s it had presided over a massive urban renewal and slum clearance programme, which had brutally transformed the city centre and broken up natural working class inner city communities, sending thousands of people to the high rise flats in the overspill estates on the perimeter of the city. The dramatic failure of that policy, and the tenants' rejection of it, turned many voters against Labour. Allied to that, the repairs and maintenance service given by the authority's workforce was extremely bad and Labour suffered for its failure to improve its performance. The city had virtually become a 'slumlord'. Also at this time in the late 1960s, Labour was a typical inner city party machine – organisationally and politically bankrupt. It was short of money, members and organisation. Many of its sitting councillors were old, patronising and out of touch with their constituents. As a former councillor admitted, the party should have got rid of many of them but didn't. So the electorate did it for them.

Labour's vices were the Liberals' virtues. They were young, energetic, hardworking and they seemed to care about people. And they were transformed by a future leader, Trevor Jones, into a phenomenally successful electoral machine. The Liberals persuaded many people in Liverpool who voted Labour nationally to vote Liberal locally. And the Liberals did well where the turnout was high. With a variety of highly successful campaigning techniques the Liberals got out their voters and won their seats. The Liberal's theme was community politics – giving the voters what they wanted. And in this they were especially able to exploit Labour's achilles heel – the condition of the city's housing – paying detailed attention to tenants' complaints and making sure officials did something about them. The Liberals took many Labour voters. But they took even more Conservative voters, many of whom were members of the skilled working class who, in other cities, where religion did not play such a part in political affiliation, might have been typical Labour voters.

Coalitions, politics and policies: the lost decade

But the Liberals' success imposed a price on the city because they were in many ways a party of protest who, when in office, had difficulty delivering a coherent set of policies for the whole city. Partly they did not want to. Under Trevor Jones the Liberals set about securing themselves a permanent social and political base in the city. They did it essentially by capturing votes where the other two parties were weakest. Labour voters lived in the inner city and council house ghettoes. The Conservatives lived in the upmarket, suburban home owners belt. The Liberals voters lived in the ring of Edwardian and Victorian terraced houses in the areas between those two. Housing became the key to politics in the city, as the Liberals identified as their power base the private renters, and the new and would-be home owners – the skilled working classes and lower middle classes.

The Liberals were given a perfect weapon in the 1974 Housing Act. Urban renewal and slum clearance were out, rehabilitation was in. And government money was available to pay for it. As one official remarked, Trevor Jones and the 1974 Act were made for each other. And he used it perfectly, developing a private sector renewal strategy which concentrated resources in an elaborate set of housing action areas with a massive improvement grant programme, a municipal build-for-sale programme, with housing associations and later housing cooperatives being given a major role. And much of the property lay in actual or potential Liberal wards.

Much of this was done at the expense of the public sector, especially the post-war high rise flats, which had few Liberal voters and was starved of funds. The 1930s cottage estates, which were rapidly upgraded, were an exception. These were frequently sold off in the major council house sales programme and again proved fertile territory for Liberal votes. But council house rents were allowed to rise as the Liberals subsidised them by the minimum amount from the rates. The municipal house building programme and the tenement rehousing programme were gradually abandoned. A huge backlog of repairs developed. The housing strategy was one-legged only. The local authority officers who had developed the private sector renewal strategy never intended that it would operate at the expense of the public sector. But party politics guaranteed that it was. As Labour did before them, and would do after them, the Liberals used housing policy partly to meet genuine housing need and diversify the housing stock, but partly with an eye on the votes. As the in-joke went, the Liberals only had one housing strategy – to build houses for sale in Labour wards and houses for rent in Tory wards.

This became crucial to Labour's battle with the Government later in the 1980s. Ideological disputes about housing policy divided the parties in the city and they were to divide the city and the Government as well. Labour's attachment to municipal housing, and its rejection of the mixed-economy approach, contributed directly to its estrangement from the Liberals in the 1970s but, more importantly, from the Conservative Government in the 1980s. And it fed the growing ideological dispute between them.

This was equally true of the other main plank of the Liberals' programme in the 1970s, its attempts to hold down the rates at the cost of expenditure on local services, primarily in an effort to capture the Liberals' constituency of small businesses, shopkeepers and the new property owning classes. The record of the Liberal party in limiting rate rises caused enormous, if unintended, financial difficulties for the city in the 1980s, when under the Conservative Government's new grant system, the city's spending record in the 1970s became the basis of cuts in financial support. Local ideological conflict over housing and spending in the 1970s sowed the seeds of a national confrontation in the 1980s.

In a different way, this was also true of another feature of coalition politics in the 1970s. The Liberals were successful in the two areas of housing and the rates because they were pursuing policies that were broadly attractive to the rump Conservative party on the council. And they could count on their votes to provide an informal, if imperfect, coalition. But the coalition worked far less well in other areas. The problem was, that between 1974 and 1983 no single party had an absolute majority on the council. And in four of those years when they were the largest party, Labour refused to take control of the council because it was unwilling to be a minority administration (see table 1). The decade was dominated by minority administrations, primarily Liberal, who could never be sure of getting sustained support for any of their policies. There was never any certainty about who would rule the city, which policies would be consistently pursued or which political deals would stick. This political uncertainty created bureaucratic uncertainty, and local officials

Table 1: Party Composition and Control of Liverpool City Council 1973–1984

	Labour	Liberal	Conservative	Party control
1973*	42	48	9	–
1974	42	47	10	Liberal
1975	42	43	14	Liberal
1976	42	40	17	†Labour
1977	42	40	17	†Labour (no election)
1978	40	35	24	†Liberal
1979	46	30	23	†Labour
1980	40	38	21	†Liberal
1981	40	38	21	†Liberal (no election)
1982	42	36	21	†Liberal
1983	51	30	18	†Labour
1984	58	28	13	†Labour

* The new council started in 1974, but the first elections to it were held in 1973.
† Labour the largest single party.

found it virtually impossible to carry out medium-term planning with any guarantee of finding political support. It was a recipe for confusion, delay and drift.

The price of this failure was that many major problems were never faced. The secondary school system was never reorganised because the three parties could never agree to a single plan. And until 1985 the secondary sector remained a patchwork of selective, comprehensive and church schools which provided thousands more places than required, and was terribly expensive to run. Also the primary school system was not rationalised because no party was willing to take the electoral risk of closing down popular, but inefficient, small local schools. This was especially true of the Liberals, whose community politics philosophy made it dangerous for them to alienate voters in marginal wards by shutting schools. The polytechnic system is too expensive because it is on a split site, spread all over the city. But again the parties could never agree on a single site. Further education has too many separate colleges which no administration could or would close. Large tracts of land in the city centre were left empty because the parties could not agree whether to develop them for industry, commerce or housing.

Equally, the council failed to face up to problems in the services which were delivered by blue collar unions. The Liberals were never able to reorganise the inefficient and poorly managed direct labour organisation which maintains the council houses, because Labour would ally with the unions and exploit it electorally. Council house tenants suffered the consequences of rotten services. Similarly, the Liberals were unable to reorganise the expensive and inefficient refuse collection service because of union opposition and lack of party support. The failure to achieve reorganisation finally led the Liberals to attempt privatisation of the service in 1982, but they could not get this passed either. Labour was prevented from tackling the problems by their ties with the unions.

The city's failure to rationalise these services, means that many now cost more and are worse than those in other cities which have had long periods of Labour control, like Manchester or Sheffield. In the Government's view, this lies at the heart of the Liverpool's current financial problems. Whether this is entirely true is another matter, as we shall see. But the demoralising impact of ten years' paralysis upon the politicians and officers cannot be understated. It was a crucial lost decade for the city. The council's inability to get a coherent strategy for the city as it was undergoing massive social change and economic decline and the unwillingness to take the difficult decisions necessary to provide reduced services for a declining population, left an extraordinarily difficult legacy for any party running the city in the mid-1980s. Decline would have been difficult to manage if the city had had enlightened leadership. That it had to endure such political incoherence instead seemed a cruel stroke of fate.

Labour and the new militancy

The final piece in the jigsaw was the Liverpool Labour party itself. During the past ten years the ideological centre of gravity of the party has been shifting from the centre to the far left. By 1985 Liverpool has become the jewel in the crown of the Militant Tendency, even though the Tendency does not have an actual majority in the Labour party. The shift is partly a matter of generational change. The membership of the party is different in the 1980s to what was in the 1970s. And their politics are different.

Throughout the 1970s, the old guard, right-wing Catholic faction were a powerful minority force in the Labour group. Even as late as 1978 they were able to stage a brief coup and depose the existing old left leader, John Hamilton, and replace him with their own candidate, Eddie Roderick. But the party activists in the city immediately revolted against the group and forced them to overturn the policy and reinstate Hamilton. That was the last gasp of the right and marked the rise of the new left. And it also marked a shift of power away from the council group to the district Labour party in the city. The eventual complete control that the district Labour party and its executive committee took over the Labour council group in the 1980s, was critical when the final confrontation with the Conservative government came in 1985.

In fact, the Liverpool Labour party had been edging to the left since the early 1970s. In 1972 the ruling Labour group had split, with 21 Labour councillors refusing to support the Labour leadership's decision to capitulate on the Conservative Government's Housing Act and raise the council rents. However, the centre right, with Bill Sefton leading, got the rises through. But the event traumatised Labour and made many decide that in future the council group had to be made much more responsible to the party activists and the unions in the city. Also through the 1970s the failures of the party – the poverty of its organisation, the poor quality of many of its councillors, its lack of contact with the community, the demoralisation of being replaced by the young Liberals, and especially its failure to develop a coherent response to the rapid economic decline of the city – began to catch up with it.

From the late 1970s, a new breed of activist began to join the Liverpool Labour party, filling the vacuum left by a generation of inadequate representatives. They were younger, more willing to work hard, more committed, more ideological and often, although not always, members of the Militant Tendency. The process of change was encouraged by other factors. Many were moving into the party from the trade union movement as they realised that isolated economic struggles over factory closures and redundancies in the 1970s were insufficient, and a broader political strategy was needed. Many were moving to the left in dissatisfaction with the failures of the Labour Government in the late 1970s. Others were reacting against the right and Thatcherism after 1979.

At the same time there was an important shift in the power of the unions within the Labour party. As the traditional industries – the car factories, the docks, transportation – declined, their unions lost ground and with it some power in the party. By contrast, the local authority public sector unions, representing the only growth sector in the city's economy in the mid 1970s, began to assume greater significance. The white-collar union, the National & Local Government Officers Association, for example, became more important politically. And so did the Militant dominated General, Municipal, Boilermakers & Allied Trades Union, which represented many blue collar, manual workers in the local authority. These two largest local authority unions played a crucial role in the city's confrontation with the Government over its budget in the 1980s. Their pressure to protect jobs made it extremely difficult for the Labour council to back down when faced by the most severe sanctions the Government and the law could impose.

These changes revitalised the Labour party and, in particular, made the local authority, both as an employer and as an institution which should be responding to local economic decline, much more central politically to Labour. And they were underwritten by the rise to prominence of the Militant Tendency within the party. Although it had been around for a long time on Merseyside, Militant with its full-time workers and legions of voluntary workers and 'readers', assumed increasing importance in the late 1970s. Militant is powerful in many wards and constituencies and in the district Labour party. In 1985 it almost won a majority on the executive committee of the district Labour party. It has about a dozen councillors in the group. And it has the deputy leader of the group in Derek Hatton.

Militant's virtues of organisation, hard work and participation, although they restricted debate within the Labour party and have many hostile critics, also galvanised the party. Membership has increased. Attendances are much higher in the wards and in the district party. Political debate has been revived, even if much of it is vitriolic and fratricidal. Militant has reinforced the reawakening of the Labour party both by bringing in many of its own members and many who are opposed to them. In fact Militant remains a minority in the party and could not get its policies through unless it got the support of the other members of the non-Militant left in the district Labour party and on the council. But it usually gets it. The power of Militant, with its commitment to revolutionary struggle, its search for a base for a workers insurrection, also encouraged the confrontation that was to come.

The power of Militant and the support it gets from the broad left has become particularly apparent since 1980 in the Labour group itself. Although the group leader remains John Hamilton, the vast majority of the group have no real connection with the politics of the 1970s, having in the main been elected since then. And they are much more on the left of the party. A major local election defeat in 1980 eliminated many of the old guard right-wingers. De-selection since then has confirmed the trend. The emergence of the Social Democratic Party attracted more of the right wing, including several former MPs, one of whom, Dick Crawshaw, was recently given a life peerage. And all five Labour MPs are now very much on the left, even though only one, Terry Fields, is actually Militant.

With this has also come a much closer connection between the left in the district Labour party and the left on the council group. The district Labour party has got in the 1980s what it never had in the 1970s: the power to actually determine the council group's policy. When adopted as candidates, members have to agree to follow district Labour party policy if elected. If they do not agree, they do not become candidates. The group does what the district Labour party tells it to do. That is why the council group remained so solidly behind the district Labour party's 'no cuts and no rate rises' policy in the 1980s. But that is no real constraint on many of the council group because as activists in the district Labour party since the 1970s, in many cases they were actually the original authors of the policy that the group should carry out the district party line. These ideological and organisational changes since the late 1970s strengthened the left in the Labour party and sharpened its appetite for, and capacity to mount, a sustained challenge to the Conservative Government in the 1980s. This can be seen nowhere more clearly than in the rising tide of budgetary militancy in recent years.

Politics and budgets, 1974–83

These basic features of Liverpool's politics during the 1970s – the Liberal attempts to build a new power base for themselves, the vagaries of coalition politics and the growing militancy of the Labour party – are perfectly illustrated by the politics of the budgetary process during the decade. Labour's stand in 1984 and 1985 can only be understood in the context of the increasingly bitter arguments about the city's finances which dominated the earlier period.

The delays, conflicts and uncertainties which characterised the 1984 and 1985 budget crises were familiar features of the previous ten years, as all parties tried to squeeze maximum political capital from the lack of a clear majority on the council. Agreed budget recommendations from the policy and finance committee were frequently rejected by the full council. Budget meetings were often abandoned without any agreement. Emergency council meetings had to be held to get any budget set. There were routine calls for financial responsibility, for the city to be taken away from politicians and given to officers, so they could produce compromise, 'save-the-city' budgets. The city came very close to entering a new financial year apparently outside the law, without having agreed a budget of any kind. If 1984 was a prelude to a troubled future, it was also the reflection of a very complicated past.

Throughout the decade the Labour party constantly argued that the Liberals were holding down the rates and underfunding the city's services to please their target voters, and their protests grew more strident over the years. Labour opposed the Liberals' refusal to spend up to the levels suggested by government grant guidelines. It opposed Liberal policy of raising council house rents above guidelines. It constantly tried to get the Liberals to increase their contributions from the rates to the housing revenue account to hold down rents. As early as 1976, Labour was attacking the Liberals' plans to pay for repairs to council housing by 'capitalising' them, that is using its capital housing allowance to pay for them and borrowing the money long term, rather than paying for them at the time by raising the rates. Labour's argument was that this helped to keep down the rates in the short term, but it would increase the long-term debt of the city which future generations would have to repay. And it also limited the amount of new housing the city could build. This became a crucial issue in the confrontation in 1984 and 1985.

The classic example of this policy was the controversial Liberals' 1975/76 budget, which has assumed intense symbolic significance in Liverpool's politics ever since. At that time, the Labour Government shifted the bias of the rate support grant towards the large urban authorities to allow them to provide increased services to cope with their special needs without having to substantially increase their rates. It brought an extra £m21 in government grant to Liverpool. But the Liberals used some of the extra money to actually cut the rates, by a penny in the pound. This provoked tremendous hostility from the Labour party and in the budget meeting its protests were so heated that it finally had to be suspended to restore order. The Liberal budget was finally carried with the support of the Conservatives after the meeting dragged on for many hours with 27 amendments being considered. This symbolic cut in the rates set the tone for Liberal financial policies, and Labour opposition to them, for the 1970s.

The conflict over budgets became particularly acute in 1977, and continued for the following two years. For example, in the previous election in May 1976 the Labour party had won the largest number of seats, but not an absolute majority on the council, and it had governed the city that year on the Liberals' budget, even though it had argued when it was passed that it was inadequate. When budget time came in April 1977, Labour tried to increase expenditure substantially and to raise the rates by over 40 per cent. Particularly significant was its plan to spend

£m8.6 from the rates to reduce council house rents. But the Liberals and Conservatives allied against the minority Labour administration, as they always did, to throw out its budget. They then imposed their own budget upon Labour, cutting the rate increase down to 20 per cent.

Exactly the same thing happened the following year in 1978. And Labour was left in April facing the prospect of running the city for the third year in succession with a budget it had argued was inadequate for the needs of the city. But in the May elections, Labour lost two seats on the council and, although it was still the largest party decided not to take minority control of the city again because it had not got its own budget and it was not likely to get its other policies through against the combined opposition of Liberals and Conservatives.

'No cuts in jobs and services'

But if the late 1970s marked Labour's growing disenchantment with the way the city finances were being run, the 1980/81 budget was a turning point which marked the appearance of Labour's strategy for the 1980s. At the same time as the Conservatives were sweeping away the Labour Government in the 1979 general election, Labour won parliamentary seats and made major gains on the Liverpool council, taking five seats from the Liberals and one from the Conservatives. Their forty-six seats on the council were an historic peak at that time. For the first six months of that year, Labour refused to take control of the council, because the other two parties would not allow Labour to have a majority on the committees. But eventually Labour did take control and ran the city for the rest of the year on the budget inherited from the Liberal party.

When Labour came to present its own budget the following April for the financial year 1980/81, however, the Conservative Government's cutbacks in public expenditure had begun to bite, and the city was starting to feel the effect of grant losses on its own finances. Labour was put in the position of having to raise the rates substantially, simply to compensate for the loss of Government grant and to maintain services at existing levels, quite apart from any plans they might have for introducing their own policies and expanding provision. Its budget needed a rate rise of over 50 per cent.

But the crucial feature of the budget debate was that the first amendment to the Labour budget was not moved in the usual way by the opposition parties but by a member of the Labour group itself, the Militant councillor, Derek Hatton. To the obvious consternation of the Labour leaders on his front benches, and the delight of the opposition parties, Hatton moved an amendment which changed the face of politics in Liverpool. It accepted the need for increased council spending but argued that it should not be paid for by a large rate increase because 'the responsibility for the plight of the city lies squarely in the lap of the Government.' The rates should be increased not by 50 per cent but by 13 per cent only, which would cover the cost of inflation and the costs of the new services Labour was planning. But there should be 'no cuts in jobs and services'. Instead, the council should unite with the Labour and trade union movement 'to fight for the money needed from the Government.' Hatton's move caused anger on the Labour benches and the amendment, which was seconded by another Militant councillor, was defeated. Only nine Labour councillors voted for it. The Liberals abstained. But there was to be no going back. That Militant 'statement of principle' would reappear to shape all of Labour's future behaviour.

The Liberals naturally attempted to make political capital out of Labour's discomfort, as well as attacking the swingeing rate rise. But the fact was that Government policy had created the problem by cutting the financial support it was giving to local authorities. Even the Liberal alternative budget, without any of Labour's new spending proposals would have needed a 42 per cent rate increase just to maintain services at existing levels. The impact of Government reductions can be seen by comparing that rise with the previous five Liberal budgets. Between 1974 and 1979 the Liberals had actually reduced the rates by 2 per cent one year and raised them by 4 per cent, 20 per cent, 6 per cent and 23 per cent respectively in succeeding years. A new phase in Liverpool's budgetary politics had begun.

This was also true of the way in which Labour finally got its budget passed. Liberal and Conservative opposition to the 50 per cent rate rise was bitter and after nine hours of argument, the first council meeting broke up in disarray without any rate being set as the opposition voted down Labour's budget. An emergency full council meeting was held the following week. Labour proposed the same budget, which the opposition tried to cut back to a 37 per cent rate rise. But they could not agree between themselves how to do it. In particular the Liberals were not willing to support the Conservative plan to cut the rate rise by substantially increasing council house rents.

As deadlock again occurred, Labour tried to postpone making a rate until after the forthcoming council elections in May, when the financial year would already be in its second month. But the opposition vetoed that idea. The meeting was then suspended while the various coalitions tried to get some agreement. In the end the Liberals simply split on Labour's budget. Eleven of them voted with the Conservatives against it. But the Liberal leadership abstained on the vote and allowed Labour's 50 per cent rate rise to carry.

Although they had the combined votes to defeat Labour, the Liberals were not willing to agree to the Conservative proposals for large rent rises, because it would have damaged them when they were fighting Labour in council house wards. In the final analysis Trevor Jones gave in to Labour because he was not willing to see the city without a budget which, as he said, would mean it would be: 'without resources, its supplies cut, the banks withholding money and eventually leading to an even higher rate.' In 1980 interpretations of the legality of entering a financial year without setting a rate set were clearly different than in 1984. And the Labour party got its first budget for the city through the council.

But as the Militant councillors had warned, the party was punished by the electorate the following month for this massive rate rise. Labour lost six seats, the largest loss ever sustained by the two major parties at that time. And Militant were never to forget the election disaster because of that large rate rise. Even in 1985 faced with municipal and personal bankruptcy, the memory was too powerful to let them change their stance. And this 1980 defeat marked another turning point. Derek Hatton took the Militant strategy to the district Labour party later that year to get it endorsed as group policy. By this time Militant was powerful enough in the district party to make sure that provocative slogan became official Labour policy from 1981 onwards. Its commitment to 'no cuts in jobs and services and no rent and rate rises to compensate for Tory cuts' guaranteed there would be some kind of confrontation between Liverpool and the Government.

Labour would not risk election defeat again by raising the rates to run the city, and allowed the Liberals to run it for the next three years. Each year Labour proposed some variation of its argument that in an area of high unemployment, the council should not make cuts in services or increase rates but should mobilise the local authority trade unions to prepare for 'the inevitable confrontation with the Government that will arise from these proposals and prepare a mass publicity campaign explaining to the people of Liverpool why this line of action is necessary.' Of course, each year the proposal got defeated. But each year the language became more strident as Liberal-Conservative coalitions, in Labour's eyes, competed with each other to produce the smallest rate rises to impress the voters, but at the same time to do the national Tories' dirty work and make the people of Liverpool pay for the Government cuts with increased rates. All this time Labour's resentment of the Government's policies, and their opponents' willingness to cooperate, was growing and making the confrontation more likely.

The final act of the Liberal Conservative coalition was the 1983/84 budget, which the Labour party inherited when it took control of the city after its council election victory in May 1983. Once more it had been difficult to get that budget passed, because the Liberals and Conservatives could not agree how to cut the Liberals' proposed spending. The original budget meeting again had to be abandoned after eight hours of squabbling between the two. A second emergency council meeting was called a week later. After much tactical voting and manoeuvring, the Conservatives finally managed to force down the Liberals' proposed expenditure to £m218. But the Government had set a spending limit for that year of £m212. In order to avoid losing grant by spending beyond that figure, the Liberals later in April 1983 simply said that they would get expenditure down to that figure of £m212 by making £m6 worth of savings during the financial year. But they did not say how that would be done. In fact, after Labour won the council election in May it ran the city on the Liberal budget during 1983/84. But spending ran far beyond £m212 and caused a large deficit at the end of the financial year. And that became the point of departure for Labour's confrontation with the Government in 1984 and afterwards.

The convoluted politics of the decade had contributed to Labour's growing militancy over the city's financial problems. Despite controlling the city on four occasions between 1974 and 1983, Labour had only been able to set one of the ten budgets, and that only with some Liberal help.

The rest had been inherited from or imposed upon them, by the Liberal-Conservative coalition. In four of the ten years, Labour had given up control of the city because it could not get its budget passed. All the other nine budgets had been set by the Liberals with Conservative support. The two parties competed for the electorate's vote by trying to keep the rates down. But they always voted together in the end.

The real difference between them was that the Conservatives, who could not hope to win wards with large numbers of council house tenants, were always willing to balance the books by raising council rents. The Liberals, who hoped to compete for the council tenants' vote, were always reluctant to raise the rents at budget time just before the elections, even though they frequently raised them afterwards. Throughout the decade, Labour became increasingly frustrated at the Liberals' refusal to spend on services. After 1979, when the Conservatives' new grant system trapped the city because of its historically low levels of spending under the Liberals, Labour's anger could not be contained. And the increasing power of Militant in the party in the late 1970s helped to focus that anger almost exclusively on the budget issue.

The actors

By 1983 the personalities who were to dominate the budget crisis had already emerged. On the Labour side, although the policy had been determined by an increasingly powerful and Militant district Labour party after 1980, the two key figures who made the running were Derek Hatton and Tony Byrne. The two could not be more different. Hatton was the flamboyant and controversial deputy-leader of the Labour group, a prominent member of the Militant Tendency who was acquiring an increasing national audience and who had ambitions to a Parliamentary career. Hatton was something of a public orator who closely identified with the miners' leader, Arthur Scargill, and saw many parallels between the miners' and Liverpool's struggle against Thatcherism.

Hatton had first sponsored the Militant 'no cuts in jobs and services' strategy through the Labour party. But his strength in the Labour party rested on his ability to fire up the party faithful and the manual trade unions, as well as aggravate the opposition parties, rather than on any understanding or grip he had of financial policy. Hatton also enjoyed an extravagant life style which constantly earned him the attacks of the Liberal party, and which at one point led to an investigation by the district auditor of his council expenses, as well as to enquiries by the police into allegations made by David Alton, the Liberal MP, in Parliament, about the details of a planning decision in the local enterprise zone. But the investigations never revealed anything untoward.

The policy leadership of the Labour party had essentially been taken over by another councillor, Tony Byrne. Byrne had only been elected to the council in 1980, but had rapidly risen to a position of virtual dominance in the group. Byrne's personal life style was austere and he was not interested in publicity or personal glory. He was a classic Jesuit trained Liverpudlian, whose style was to apply his logic to a problem and, having reached a solution, to refuse to be moved from it. He did not enjoy, and would not tolerate, dissenting opinions. And he could be ruthless and dogmatic. This made him a difficult ally and a more difficult opponent, as Patrick Jenkin was to discover. In three years on the council Byrne had rapidly mastered the complexities of finance, housing and the urban programme – the heart of a Labour authority's concerns. And he had written almost single-handedly the strategy of the Labour administration in these areas when it took control of the council in 1983.

At heart Byrne believed in centralised municipal solutions to deal with working class deprivation, and this made him as unpopular with many in the soft left in the Labour party, the community and the private sector, as he was to become with the Government. In two years of office his concentration of resources in the public sector alienated many groups and agencies which had been accustomed to much more generous support from the council under the Liberal regime, as well as many who wanted a more decentralised and popular style of decision-making.

Byrne entered the confrontation with the Government with a clearly defined set of political goals which he had decided were more important than his personal position. He had no fears about the consequences of his actions. His view was that at the end of the day, if it all went wrong, all the Government could do was bankrupt him and then pay him his social security! He was quite willing to take that risk to get the housing and physical environment that he believed the working class in Liverpool deserved. He was certainly willing to try to blackmail a Tory Government to do it. Byrne was not a Militant and had few larger political ambitions outside Liverpool. He was not primarily interested in confrontation for its own sake. If he could get what he wanted out of the Government without a struggle, that would suit him just as well. He knew what he wanted and was clever in getting it. He played his cards very close to his chest and shared his views reluctantly.

The senior officers advising the Labour leadership were the chief executive, Alfred Stocks, and the treasurer, Michael Reddington. Reddington was relatively new to the job and was thrust into the deep end of the confrontation. Throughout, he believed the city had a very good case against the Government and was always disappointed that his peers in the Department of the Environment simply refused to acknowledge, as fellow professionals, the problems which the grant system had caused for Liverpool. The pressures of the confrontation and sailing so close to illegality weighed heavily upon him.

Stocks was an older hand who was highly respected in the local authority world. He had been in the authority since the 1950s, the chief executive since 1973, and was long accustomed to the ways of Liverpool politics. He had spent most of his tenure of office trying to give some administrative leadership to a highly fragmented local authority in the difficult era of coalition politics. The experience of working with a majority administration with very fixed views and a determination to challenge the Government was a novel one. But he also believed the city had had a raw deal, and occasionally despaired of the way the Government was proceeding. But when professional colleagues sympathised with his troubles in Liverpool, he always replied that it was the most interesting job in local government. Like many others, he could not resist the pleasures and perversities of Liverpool politics.

By 1983, the Government had a very visible presence in Liverpool. Since the Toxteth riots in 1981, there had been a Minister for Merseyside who regularly visited the city. And he had his Task Force of about 40 civil servants and private sector managers who had learned a lot about the city. In fact, the Government was better informed about Liverpool and more intimately involved in its politics and policies, than any other city in the country outside London. And despite considerable local scepticism about the value of the Task Force, it had attracted to Liverpool especially under the first Minister for Merseyside, Michael Heseltine, a number of high quality civil servants. Its director, Eric

Sorenson, was a key player in 1984. Sorenson was one of the rising stars in the Department of the Environment, the youngest civil servant ever to reach the rank of Under-Secretary. Like many who were achieving prominence in the Department at the time, Sorenson was intellectually and emotionally attuned to the free market philosophy of the Government and unsympathetic to many of the failings of local authorities. But like Michael Heseltine himself, he was fascinated by Liverpool's politics, read the situation well and provided London with a stream of informed analysis of the moving target of the budget crisis.

But he was in some ways advising a rather clumsy Minister. Patrick Jenkin was essentially a legalist with little feel for the nuances of politics in Liverpool, who frequently handed propaganda victories to his opponents. He let matters drift early on when clever Ministerial action might possibly have diverted the course of the crisis before it got under way. The feeling persisted that Michael Heseltine, the first Minister for Merseyside, would have behaved differently. Unlike Jenkin, Heseltine had a good feel for Liverpool politics and politicians and a high reputation. An astute politician himself, Heseltine would have attempted a deal earlier on with the Labour leaders, by promising them enough money to make them at least want to play the game and preventing the financial crisis going so far. But whether even he could have done it, given the political forces in Liverpool, was unlikely.

Throughout the lost decade a series of pressures pushed Liverpool towards the crisis. The collapse of its economy as the large private firms abandoned the city ensured that unemployment and jobs – especially public sector jobs – became the central theme of its political life. The election of a Conservative Government with few political votes in Liverpool, little sympathy for declining northern cities, an ideological destation of the public sector and commitment to the private sector, increased the prospect of some form of conflict. The combination of intense local ideological disputes and chaotic responses to decline worsened the picture. The Conservative's introduction of a complicated and controversial grant system brought the city to the edge of the precipice. And the re-emergence of a 'hard left' Labour party, supported by powerful local authority unions, threatened to push the city over it. Liverpool's budget crisis was like a Greek tragedy. Its fate was determined as the play opened. The actors merely made sure it met it.

THE OPENING ROUND: LIVERPOOL AGAINST WHITEHALL – May 1983 - September 1984

2

The roots of the confrontation between Liverpool and the Government lay deep in the politics and policies of the 1970s. But it became inevitable after the Liverpool Labour party won its victory in the local elections in May 1983. This gave a clear majority to one party on the city council for the first time in a decade. And the Labour-controlled council was now in a position to carry its attack to the Conservative Government. All the next year, Liverpool's politics and its relations with the Government were dominated by a single issue, the state of the city's finances. Labour ran the city on the budget the Liberal party had left them. But as it had promised, it spent the whole period running a campaign to convince its workforce, the electorate, other Labour authorities, the national Labour leadership and the Conservative Government that its finances were unmanageable. Although there were a number of possible interpretations of the city's position, Labour finally persuaded many people that its was right. The Government never believed it. But in 1984, at least, threatened by municipal bankruptcy, it eventually conceded some ground to Liverpool's argument. The Labour council turned the conflict into a poker game in which the stakes became too high for the Government. It had other battles to fight in 1984, and in the end this was crucial.

The Labour council's case

The Labour council's argument was its financial problems could not be seen in isolation from the overall economic decline of the city and especially the Conservative Government's failure to help it. That economic decline, its aggravation by cuts in Government spending and the alleged irresponsibility of previous Liberal regimes, were Labour's justification for its political challenge to the Government. And it claimed it had got a mandate from the local electorate in May 1983 to defend existing council jobs and services, build council houses for rent, end the threat of privatisation of council services and refuse to cut local services or impose increases in rates and rents to compensate for Government cuts.

This had been Labour policy for several years. The difference now was that it argued that the combination of a large deficit caused by the inadequate Liberal budget it had inherited in May 1983, and the impact of an increasingly harsh Government grant system, meant that the city's finances were unmanageable without making 'massive' cuts in local services, or a reduction of 5,000 council jobs or a rate increase of 170 per cent. In other words, a legal, balanced budget could not be made without seriously damaging the city's economy further or worsening its social problems. Since Labour had not been elected to make the people of Liverpool pay for the Government's cuts in this way, it would not balance the city's books.

The Labour council's plan was alarmingly simple. It intended to make a deficit budget for 1984/85. This would pay for existing services plus its own new programmes, for which it claimed it had got a mandate. But it planned to raise the rates by only 9 per cent. The council's income inevitably would be far less than its expenditure and there would be a huge illegal deficit at the end of the financial year, assuming the city could keep running that long. Even if Labour dropped its new spending plans, and simply ran the services at existing levels in a 'stand still' budget, with a 9 per cent rise the city would still run out of money.

But in Labour's eyes the responsibility was not theirs, but the Government's, who by consistently cutting financial support to Liverpool since 1979 had 'stolen' £m270 from the city in four years. Labour's plan was to blackmail the Government into giving back £m30 of that money so it could balance its books. If it refused, Labour would simply bankrupt the city and allow it to collapse. The employees would lose their jobs. The schools, colleges, libraries and nurseries would be closed. The old people's and children's homes would be without staff, heating or food. Rubbish would pile up all over the city. No housing repairs would be done. The dead might not even be buried.

The city's argument with the Conservatives was part of a larger one that has been going on between national and local government since

1979. The strains that were apparent during the later years of the Labour Government in the 1970s became ruptures in the 1980s, as the Conservatives led a demoralising attack on local government and public expenditure. And with the Government's new philosophy of privatism, wealth creation and capital investment became the primary goal of urban policy at the expense of traditional social welfare policies. The concern to revive inner city economies had been an element of the Labour Government's urban programme in the mid-1970s. But it became central to the Conservatives. The private sector was once seen as part of the problem of the declining cities. In the 1980s it was to be part of the solution.

The problem with this analysis was that the private sector was abandoning Liverpool, as we have seen, at an accelerating rate; since 1979 at least 40,000 jobs had been lost. As the Labour council constantly pointed out, there was no evidence that Government measures to stimulate the private sector had done anything to slow down the city's decline. This was why the dispute about public expenditure became so bitter in Liverpool, because the second leg of the Conservative argument was that, as the private sector grew, the public sector should contract. Labour argued that since market forces were already undermining Liverpool's precarious economic base, it made no sense to cut back its public sector as well. In particular, it made no sense to limit the local authority's spending, when that would inevitably mean cuts in the workforce and higher unemployment in the city.

The Labour council was bound to reject a policy which would increase unemployment in Liverpool by a contraction of the public sector. It saw local authority services both as a necessary social support system for an increasingly impoverished community, and a valuable source of jobs which kept people from their only likely alternative – the dole. In its mind, the Liverpool Labour party was not in business to implement major cuts in services demanded by a Conservative Government. It had either to resist or resign. The Government of course had a quite different view: in the patronising words which Patrick Jenkin constantly repeated, the local authority was not 'a system of outdoor relief'. If unemployment was the price of economic growth, it would have to be paid.

But as Labour replied, the price would have to be paid twice. First the workers and their families would suffer probably lengthy unemployment, and whatever contribution they made to the social welfare would be lost. But the Government would pay a price as well. There would be the usual costs of keeping people unemployed – the loss of revenue from income tax and national insurance payments, plus all the unemployment benefits it would have to pay – which might add up to two-thirds of the cost of the original wages. But the added irony of the Government's grant system was that if the city cut its workforce, it would also get back more than twice the amount saved in Government grant. As Liverpool reduced its wages bill and got closer to the expenditure target given to it by the Government, the money that would have been taken away in grant penalties for spending over its set limit would be given back to it. This would mean Liverpool's rates could be held down. But the Government and the taxpayer would be heavily subsidising them. It would cost them more to keep people unemployed, than it did for the local authority to keep them in work. The Government replied that the respective contribution of taxpayers and the ratepayers was not an issue in this particular argument. But this was a narrow form of social accounting at best. And the Labour council would not accept it. It believed the Government's policy was flawed and vulnerable to a direct political attack. And it spent its first year in office carrying one out.

Selling the argument to the workforce

Labour knew that to take its argument beyond the city and challenge the Government, it needed the support of its own workforce and the voters in Liverpool. In fact, persuading the local workforce and their unions proved a simple task. The experience of Liberal control of the council in the 1970s had forced them into the arms of Labour. Throughout their decade of power, in order to hold down spending and limit rate rises, the Liberals had cut the authority's workforce by about 4,000 down to about 30,000. But they had done this not with a redundancy, but with a natural wastage, policy. And this inevitably had arbitrary and disruptive impacts upon staffing levels in different local authority departments. Through the late 1970s this policy had created rising frustrations and tensions between the council and the unions. The election of the Thatcher Government in 1979 only increased local union fears that the national trend would reinforce Liberal practices and that year they formed a powerful joint shop stewards committee from all local authority unions to resist further pressures for job losses.

Matters came to a head for the Liberals during the 1980s in conflicts with two major unions, the white collar National & Local Government Officers Association and the blue collar General, Municipal, Boilermakers & Allied Trades Union. These two unions had different, conflicting political traditions. NALGO was a traditionally conservative 'bosses' union which, despite its radicalisation at national level over public expenditure cuts, and its left wing leadership in Liverpool, was always regarded as an uncertain ally by the Labour council. The 'General and Municipal', by contrast, was an old fashioned, manual workers' local authority union. It had strong Militant leadership in key branches and at shop steward level and was very powerful in the district Labour party.

But in their later years in office the Liberals managed to alienate both these unions. In 1978 there had been a prolonged social workers' strike over salary structures, which had both radicalised union members and left bitter memories of the Liberals as employers. In 1982 a dispute over regrading policy for secretarial staff, which would effectively have held down wages, provoked a typists' strike which lasted over nine months. The strike disrupted much of the work of the authority and caused tremendous bitterness. And with Derek Hatton playing a very visible part in the dispute, Labour was able to build on the conflict, to break NALGO's weakening links with the Liberals and bring it over to Labour's side.

At the same time that the typists' dispute was radicalising the white collar workers, the Liberals were having union difficulties elsewhere. They were trying to save money by privatising the notoriously expensive and inefficient refuse collection service. This provoked another traumatic dispute with 'General and Muncipal' members, the binmen. Their union mounted a major campaign to resist privatisation and the plan eventually had to be postponed by the Liberals. But the attempt made a key group of manual workers sensitive to any threat of job loss. Labour's election campaign in 1983 in defence of 'jobs and services', and its attacks on the Liberals, struck an immediate chord with these two largest and most powerful local authority unions and probably helped them to gain control of the council. And their leadership, with encouragement from the Labour party, played a crucial part in the elaborate campaign the following year to get the council's message about the budget crisis across to shop stewards and workers.

And Labour's year long campaign with its workforce and unions worked. When the time came to support the council in the spring of 1984, nearly all the major unions delivered substantial majorities in favour of Labour's plan for a deficit budget. The National Union of Teachers was the only one to oppose it. But even this normally conservative union was evenly split; at a mass meeting of 2,000 teachers, the union rejected Labour's stand by just over a hundred votes. The Government also regarded the unions as a key group and the most vulnerable one in the triumvirate of party, voters and workers. Its own propaganda campaign constantly tried to dislodge them from Labour's side by emphasising the price the workforce would have to pay if the council finally refused to raise enough money to keep the city running. But the triumvirate held.

Persuading the voters

Labour also began a major propaganda effort to convince the Liverpool public at the end of 1983. Before then most people knew little about the issue. The council had focused its attention on the workforce. Anyway stories of impending industrial and financial disasters were familiar on depressed Merseyside. The preliminary skirmishes between the parties on the council had made little public impact either. Much to the anger of the opposition parties, who claimed it was a Militant Tendency propaganda machine paid for by the rates, Labour set up a central support unit to orchestrate the presentation of its case.

The unit started its campaign with a 'Merseyside in Crisis' demonstration at which leaders of Labour's left including Tony Benn and David Blunkett addressed 20,000 people. It staged elaborate sets of forty public meetings, in April and June 1984, which were attended by over 5,000 people. It ran a rally on the eve of the meeting attended by over a thousand activists and a mass demonstration of over 25,000 people on the day of the budget meeting in April 1984. It ran a petition in support of the city, which got 20,000 signatures during the spring. And it ran the election campaign in April 1984, which focused almost exclusively on the budget. And again the campaign worked, with a turnout of 51 per cent, and another Labour victory.

Labour's campaign successfully politicised the budget crisis, turning a complicated, financial argument into a simple choice between the Government's version of the story and their own. It tied together the interests of the council workers, the consumers of local services, and of the domestic and commercial ratepayers. And it won the propaganda battle for Labour. The campaign persuaded enough people that the Labour council was right and that major cuts in services and jobs or large rate rises were the only options. And it deflected attention away from the argument the Government wanted to make – that the city was expensive and inefficient and could easily provide existing services for less money without major financial problems. Just as the unions supported the Labour party when it most needed it, in the spring of 1984 the voters did so, with crucial effect. The extent of local electoral support Labour got for its stand in 1984 played a major part in getting an eventual resolution.

Ironically, in view of the common criticism of the secretiveness of Liverpool's Labour party, it made a major effort to publicise its own case. But it is less clear whether the campaign ever sought to present the budget problem as a series of options between which the public might choose. Every effort was made to put Labour's side. But little was made to explore the alternatives between rate rises of 170 per cent, 5,000 redundancies or a deficit budget. The Labour leadership decided to dramatise the city's position and present stark alternatives rather than to cloud the political issues by discussing different ways in which the budget might be balanced. Labour had good political grounds for rejecting any intermediate positions. But they were still given little public exposure.

Indeed a key feature of this confrontation was that, despite the publicity campaign, very few people in the Labour group – let alone the opposition parties, the workforce, or the public – actually knew the city's exact financial position and the options open to it. Partly, this was inevitable. Local government finance and budgets are complicated and have become increasingly esoteric in the 1980s. But also it was intentional. The detailed information necessary to make a judgement was never released but carefully held in the hands of Labour's finance chief, Tony Byrne, precisely so that alternative strategies could not emerge. This allowed Byrne to choose the ground for the confrontation with the Government just as he saw fit.

By the early part of 1984, the Liverpool Labour party had begun to successfully mobilise its workforce and other people in the city. And it seemed that they would have their support for some kind of confrontation with the Government about the city's finances. But if it was to get anywhere with its argument it knew it would also have to persuade people outside Liverpool that it had a case – especially the national Labour Party and later the Conservative Government. And they might both see things differently from the Labour council and its supporters.

Selling the argument nationally

At the beginning of 1984 Liverpool's strategy was not very well-known outside the city. The Government was not paying very much attention to it. Nor was the national Labour Party, which was more concerned with devising a strategic response to the Government's planned rate-capping legislation in 1985, designed to limit the money which selected high-spending Labour authorities could spend. But in the end, Liverpool embarrassed both of them and forced them to shift their ground. Through the spring and summer of 1984, the Liverpool Labour party's campaign inside and outside the city, guaranteed that Liverpool dominated discussion of local politics in Parliament and the media, as the twists and turns of the tale led the players into constitutionally uncharted waters.

Labour was convinced that in the end the Government would not risk the political consequences of the collapse of the city's economy and services. They had no other plan than to press the argument as far as possible and see where it led them. They had no alternative strategies and no apparent fallback position. Many Labour politicians outside Liverpool regarded this as a high-risk strategy at best, and at worst as 'revolutionary defeatism.' But a potent combination of analysis and rhetoric, fuelled by the adrenalin of the mass campaign, got the Labour group into a position from which it could not retreat without personal or political humiliation. The Quaker Labour leader, John Hamilton, for example, confessed that, despite his worst fears, he could live with bankruptcy more easily than he could with the charge of treachery which would inevitably follow if Labour gave in. Liverpool simply had to keep going forward with the struggle. It did not know what else to do.

In fact, getting people outside the city to accept their argument was much tougher for the Labour council. Their campaign opened with a letter from Derek Hatton to all Labour MPs in November 1983 claiming that Liverpool could not be left to fight the Government on its own but that there must be 'a common strategy and campaign involving all the Labour councils.' During the following months, Liverpool spokesmen carried that argument around many local authorities and local Labour parties trying to get support for their stand. They also took it to the Party's important local government conference at Nottingham in February 1984. But their plan for illegality met with resistance at that conference, even from those who were sympathetic to Liverpool's problems as well as to the idea of a campaign of direct action on local government finance.

Labour's national leader, Neil Kinnock, was especially alarmed by the prospect of a Militant-led Liverpool locked into an illegal battle with the Conservative Government. He reminded a divided conference that official Party policy was that councillors should stay in office and try to minimise the effect of any cuts. John Cunningham, the Party's national spokesman on local government, also emphasised the need for Labour authorities to stay within the law, warning Liverpool it could not expect the automatic support of the national Party. 'We should not become obsessed with Liverpool' he said. 'Many other councils are also in difficulty. Trying to bring about confrontation is not the way forward. We will not give Liverpool a blank cheque for what they want to do without telling all of their financial details first. So far they have not given us the financial information we have asked for.' John Cunningham clearly did not believe Liverpool's specific argument about its budget problems, let alone in the general principle of law breaking.

Nor were other important local leaders at the conference much more impressed. Despite the call of the London leader, Ken Livingston, for defiance of rate-capping, the chairman of the conference, David Blunkett, argued that the time was not ripe for law-breaking and that the public had first to be persuaded that the law was bad. He was also sceptical of Liverpool's claim that other local authorities should support them in their stand. Liverpool would be heard but, 'we don't want to pretend we can be of help if we can't. There will be a great deal of sympathy for Liverpool. But the other left-wing authorities are not in the same position as Liverpool so there is no way they can take the same stand. We're not going to stab them in the back, but we'll have to tell them that if they can stick with us then they should.'

At the beginning of 1984, Liverpool was not getting whole-hearted support from the Labour movement which was worried that the city's strident, illegal strategy would completely backfire and damage the more carefully planned, national campaign against rate-capping in 1985. Labour's national leadership was growing distinctly uneasy about the political impact of such a confrontation. Some senior members of the national executive committee, including the party chairman and Liverpool MP Eric Heffer, were anxious to defy the leadership by declaring sympathy for Liverpool's stand. But Kinnock stood firm against illegality which he thought a great threat to the national party's election image.

Privately, John Hamilton believed Kinnock and the national leadership were completely out of touch with the mood in Liverpool. Wrecked by the general election disaster of 1983, lagging behind the Social Democratic Party in much of the south, trying to reconstruct Party unity as well as its organisational machine, the national Party simply could not understand Labour's position in Liverpool. It was fresh from local and national election success, not failure, in 1983 and anxious to press on aggressively with its opposition to Conservative policies which had hit the city so badly. The national leadership, in turn, thought that Liverpool was recklessly endangering the national Party's chances of ever mobilising support against the Conservative Government.

The national leadership's failure to support Liverpool, indeed Kinnock's refusal to even visit the city, drove a wedge between the national and local party that never closed. The national leadership found Liverpool's behaviour almost as incomprehensible and as difficult to deal with as the Conservative Government did. The political sub-culture of the Liverpool Labour party with its aggressive, Militant and 'workerist' overtones made it different from many other local parties. And just as the city played little part on the larger national economic stage, Liverpool had little status in the traditional hierarchy of national Labour Party politics. Only one of them, Eric Heffer, had a major role.

Politically, and economically, Liverpool was estranged from the national mainstream. That sense of isolation and the resulting frustration, which was a product of the city's decline, fuelled the Labour council's struggle. It was not only an attack on the Government. It was also Liverpool's stand against the larger world outside. And national elites did not quite know how to handle it. But later in February 1984, the council managed to get Labour's junior spokesman on the environment, Jack Straw, to come to Liverpool and look at the financial position. And they partly persuaded him. Straw left to report back to Kinnock agreeing 'The picture that I was given of the inheritance left to Labour last May by the previous Liberal-Tory administration was worse than I had expected.' A window of opportunity had opened for Liverpool. The local party had begun to get the national leadership at least to take its problems seriously.

Persuading the Government

At the same time, in early 1984 Liverpool opened its campaign to persuade the Government. The day after Straw had visited them, at their own request, Hatton, Byrne and Hamilton led a small group to meet Patrick Jenkin in London to argue that the Government should find £m30 to cover the city's intended budget deficit. Patrick Jenkin was not as understanding as Jack Straw. He flatly refused to discuss the possibility of more money for Liverpool. His reply in February 1984, was the one he consistently made until later in July. Liverpool was not unique in facing tough political choices. The principles of the grant system applied to all authorities. He had no power to make special rules for the city. In fact Liverpool's grant reduction was less than some other authorities that year. Labour had inherited a tight budgetary position in 1983 from the Liberals. But they had aggravated their problems by not merely failing to make the savings on which that budget was based, but by actually increasing expenditure.

Equally, he argued, Liverpool's claims were incompatible with its own national leadership's view that a standstill budget could be financed by a 60 per cent rate increase. And he suggested they make that kind of rate rise. He admitted the city did have 'exceptional social problems' but the Government had recognised these with a variety of special programmes for Liverpool. Its rate support grant was certainly declining, but it was Government policy to reduce the proportion of local spending supported by the national taxpayer. This applied to all authorities, not just Liverpool. The bottom line was that the council was 'proposing to spend money it hasn't got and is asking us to go outside the rules to make it up. That is not acceptable. We must apply the same rules evenhandedly to all authorities'. Labour returned empty-handed on the train to Liverpool. The next day Tony Byrne described Jenkin as 'a very bad man'. It was going to be a long struggle for Labour to get what it wanted out of the Government. But it was prepared for it.

But the failure of this first meeting with Jenkin in February 1984 intensified national criticism of Liverpool's stance and the fears about its consequences. Those fears were compounded when the claim gradually leaked out that at the meeting, Derek Hatton had threatened violence on the streets of Liverpool and outside Patrick Jenkin's own home, if the Government did not give the city its extra money. Despite Liverpool's protestations, these threats allowed Jenkin to claim 'the whole thing is designed to create confrontation with the Government and overthrow the Thatcher administration. They have never made any secret of that'. The Prime Minister herself condemned Hatton in Parliament. 'The threats of violence will not help Liverpool, indeed will do Liverpool great damage.' she said. 'I hope nothing further will be heard about them and nothing further will be done.' Whatever Derek Hatton had said to Patrick Jenkin, it gave the Government a flavour of the Labour leadership's style. It raised the temperature of the argument and made a future compromise a little less likely.

Labour's defections and increased uncertainty

By the spring of 1984, the significance and risks of Liverpool's plan were becoming increasingly obvious. Local people were by now well aware of the problem. But national elites had also begun to see where it might lead. And neither the Conservative nor the Labour Party leadership liked the look of the way things were developing. For different reasons, they were both very suspicious of Liverpool's argument and its plan. They did not believe that the city's financial position was as bad as the local politicians were claiming. And they certainly did not think that threatening to bankrupt the city was the right way of dealing with it. And neither national party wanted the political embarrassment this potential local suicide would cause them. On the other hand, they were not sure at this point whether Liverpool Labour actually had the nerve, or the votes, to carry out its threat.

But national attention once again focused on Liverpool itself as 29 March, budget day, loomed nearer and with it the prospect of municipal bankruptcy and the breakdown of all local services. The position inside the Labour group was obviously crucial. Labour only had a slender majority of three on the council and there were well-known political divisions between the old guard right wing of the group and the broad left and Militant councillors. As the legal, political and financial pressures on individual councillors mounted, it was obvious that self-interest or ideology could produce enough defections for Labour to lose its majority. There had been rumours to that effect in the city for weeks. Indeed, there was tacit agreement amongst the party's critics – the Government, the national Labour leadership, the local opposition parties – that it was only pursuing the confrontation because it knew that defections doomed it to eventual failure, while guaranteeing Liverpool the reputation of having resisted the Tory Government to the last.

The long predicted split finally came on 7 March when six right-wingers announced their defections in the local press, leaving the enraged Labour group to discover the fact on the front page of the Liverpool Echo, as they sat in a full council meeting, listening to the taunts of their opponents. The six rebels were not prepared to support a deficit budget which jeopardised the livelihood of council employees when none of them had ever been shown any official figures about the city's financial position. A furious Derek Hatton threatened that the rebels would be 'dealt with by the party, they will be dealt with by the trade union movement and the vast majority of people in this city'. They would become 'political lepers'. But the leading rebel, Eddie Roderick, replied 'Labour have taken on the Government and they have lost. I am not going to be intimidated by threats from people I see as extremists'. Labour's national spokesman, John Cunningham, with obvious relief praised the rebels for being 'brave and sensible'. The local opposition parties insisted the Labour council was equally relieved because it could now blame 'the enemy within' for saving it from a fate which it did not in fact want.

Many people now believed that Labour's bluff had been called and that it would settle down to produce some kind of legal budget. The split in the group seemed to have saved Liverpool from the immediate crisis. But people soon realised that longer-term problems remained as bad as ever. If, for example, Labour did not budge and the 'sensible six' would not support the opposition parties' budget proposals, the danger was that there would be no majority for anything in the council and the city would drift into the new financial year in April 1984 without any budget at all. If the city could survive until May, the annual council elections were due. But no one knew whether they would produce a clear majority for legality, another hung council or an increased majority for Labour, which would guarantee the passage of the deficit budget.

The prospect of an illegal or no budget raised all kinds of financial and legal issues and caused some panic amongst city and Government officials. As the senior civil servant in the city, Eric Sorenson, put it, 'We are in completely new territory. No local authority has ever sought to do anything like this before.' And no one had a clue how it would unravel. It was not legally necessary that a rate be fixed before the beginning of the financial year. But in practical terms, if the city set no rate, or an illegally low rate, it was not clear how long it would be able to continue to borrow the money in the private market that it needed to pay its debts. That would depend on the attitude of private investors towards the risk involved.

It also depended on the reserves available to the treasurer and the city's need to borrow. It not only had to borrow short term on its revenue account to pay various bills, as it waited for income to come in from rates, grants and rents. It also had accumulated long-term debts in the region of £m700 from its building programmes over the years. Each year the city had to borrow about £m190 to pay off part of those outstanding debts. This was almost as large as the total annual revenue budget. If the city could not borrow more money to pay these long term capital debts as they became due, it would have to use revenue income. If that happened, the city would run out of money very quickly indeed, and would be unable to pay any of its bills or staff.

The Government believed that initially it would have to continue to pay Liverpool its rate support grant. This would in turn encourage the Public Works Loan Board, the public lender of last resort, to continue lending to Liverpool. And the city had over 60 per cent of its loans with the Board. But it was not certain what the Board's own position would be in the longer term if the authority had no rate income, the only guarantee of any local authority's credit worthiness. The city would continue to receive income from council house tenants who paid rents and rates jointly. But these would not keep the city afloat permanently without a rate being set. Uncertainty about all these factors left both city and Government officials unsure whether the city would run out of money in a matter of weeks, or whether it could hang on for months. The real danger was that the city might slither into bankruptcy almost by default, with no one particularly intending it. That prospect began to alarm many people. But throughout, Tony Byrne stayed calm telling officials and councillors that they had to keep their nerve. He felt sure he would get Liverpool through.

There was equal uncertainty about the legal position, partly because the issues had not been tested. Under the 1967 General Rate Act any ratepayer, city stockholder or creditor could challenge the council in the High Court. The court could quash the rate and instruct councillors to fix a legal one. If they did not do so they could be fined for unlimited amounts of money and eventually imprisoned for contempt of court for up to two years. Abstention on crucial illegal votes would not absolve individual councillors from the court's judgement. Each councillor would have had to vote in favour of a legal rate. This would obviously affect the liability of the Labour rebels. If it wished, the Government itself could take legal action through the Attorney General to make the city set a legal rate. And the district auditor could initiate action, if he decided the councillors were guilty of 'wilful misconduct' in the management of the city's financial affairs and have them surcharged under the 1982 Local Government Finance Act. Each guilty councillor would be made personally liable for illegal spending. If the loss was more than £2,000, it could lead to disqualification of councillors from public office for five years, and bankruptcy if they were unable to pay the money.

Finally, if the city's basic services did collapse when it ran out of money, the Government could introduce legislation allowing it to take over the city directly and run it with commissioners. But the problems for the Government in doing that were enormous. Civil servants were appalled at the prospect of having to run Liverpool. They knew their life would be miserable. They were not impressed by the city's administration of its services. They always had difficulty with the Labour administration getting the quality of co-operation and information they wanted to make their joint programmes work. The idea of being responsible for all of the city's basic services, to say the least, alarmed them. Also, the broad role commissioners might play was quite uncertain. It was unclear how extensive their duties would be, how long they would have to stay, how they could be removed once installed. Would they stay to the next election, the next financial year or far longer until the money was sorted out? It was not clear whether they would get the necessary co-operation of the local workforce to run the city, especially if they imposed cuts in services, or made employees redundant. Nor was it known whether there would be any form of popular resistance.

The Government was becoming increasingly worried by the situation in Liverpool. The prospect of getting directly involved in running the city with commissioners, with the very high risk of making political or administrative mistakes, was very unattractive. But the Government also realised that it could not stand aside indefinitely if services in one of the country's largest cities, where there had recently been extensive civil unrest and violence, began to collapse. The attraction of leaving matters to the courts was that it distanced the Government from the immediate decision. But it could hardly deny its general involvement in Liverpool's financial problems. Nor was it enthusiastic about the uncertainty involved in leaving things to the courts, or of the possibility that legal action might make martyrs of Labour councillors and turn public opinion nationally against the Government.

Until the council made its next move, of course, the Government had no need to do anything. For the time being its plan was to remain as distant as possible from the issue, emphasising that it was the council's, not the Government's responsibility to set a rate, in the hope that the growing political isolation of the council would bring capitulation. The Government's willingness to sit on its hands alarmed some local officials, who felt it was showing a lack of common sense about the city's difficulties. Indeed, the chief executive, Alfred Stocks, was concerned that revolt was in the air in the city, and might come, if the Government continued with these tactics.

These fears were echoed by the city's church leaders. The influential Bishop of Liverpool, David Sheppard, although wholly opposed to Labour's plan, argued that behind it lay 'a cry of pain.' 'Some of us' he said 'are trying to persuade people not to abandon the rule of law and peaceful processes of change. But, if we are successful in such law abiding persuasion and they pull back from the brink, what will happen then? Will prosperous Britain heave a sigh of relief and forget about Liverpool again? Make no mistake, we are wasting the God-given resources of the nation by leaving three million people on the dole and we are breeding a dangerously bitter spirit.' Politicians, officials and church leaders were all agreed at least about one thing, the potential dangers of the situation. Violence was always a lurking possibility. And throughout the confrontation, the Bishop and his Roman Catholic counterpart, Archbishop Derek Worlock, remained in constant contact with Jenkin and Thatcher, as well as the local Labour leaders, trying to avoid that possibility and to keep the lines of communication open and with it the hope of moderate solutions. Their contribution was subtle but undeniable. Arguably it helped shape the Government's final response.

Labour presses on

Liverpool, meanwhile, turned back to Neil Kinnock for help after the city's five Labour MPs had persuaded him to meet the local leaders. But to their surprise, when the councillors arrived at the House of Commons, they found not only Kinnock, but the national general secretaries of the three major local authority unions, all of whom expressed their worries about where Liverpool was leading their local members. Labour's reply was brutal. Their finance spokesman, Tony Byrne, explained that he fully understood these worries. They presented no problem for the Labour council. But he asked each union leader to tell him the names of the thousand of their local members he should make redundant. At this point, the union leaders beat a collective exit to allow Neil Kinnock his opportunity to persuade the local politicians of the folly of their ways. He failed.

But Kinnock would not make what he called the 'idle gesture' of endorsing Liverpool's stand. He told them to get in line with party policy, administer the cuts humanely and maintain a common front for 1985. He insisted there were 'difficult but nonetheless practical budget alternatives' which the city should consider. And although he did not suggest any specific answers to Liverpool's problem, it was widely known that after Straw's inspection of the city's books, Kinnock's private office had produced an alternative budget outline which implied a 60 per cent rate rise. This was the strategy that he wanted Liverpool to follow. As Kinnock said on other occasions – better the dented shield than none at all.

But obviously Liverpool were not going to do this. And this marked the estrangement of the two sides. Throughout the struggle, many Liverpool councillors, especially the Militants, regarded the national leaders as traitors who constantly pushed unacceptable solutions on Liverpool, providing their opponents in the city with powerful arguments against them. In fact many believed that the national leadership's real worry was that if they sided with Liverpool's case for special treatment when the Conservatives were in office, they would be storing up future trouble for themselves if they ever formed a Government. This was part of the problem. Many in the Liverpool Labour party had little confidence that a future Labour Government would follow the kinds of socialist policies they wanted. Liverpool's plan was to use the struggle over the budget to first drive out Thatcher. But the struggle would only then begin for control of the Labour Government. As Tony Byrne publicly argued, it was no good just having any kind of Labour Government repeating the betrayals of its predecessors. For some in the Liverpool Labour party, a future Labour Government would be as much a potential enemy as a potential ally.

The legal warnings

After the unsuccessful meetings with Kinnock in March 1984, it was clear that Liverpool was out on its own. And the pressures on the Labour group were growing alarmingly. On 19 March the district auditor, Lesley Stanford, entered the scene by warning the councillors of the dangers they were in. If they levied an insufficient rate, the council would run out of money, be unable to borrow and there would be 'a serious breakdown.' There would be inevitable losses to the council and he would have to decide whether to charge the individual councillors involved for them. His told them that 'it would be less than helpful if I were to fail to say at this stage that I should find it difficult to see how the deliberate making of an inadequate rate could be anything other than wilful misconduct'. But he did not give them a deadline for action. And they did not take him very seriously.

These warnings were underlined in a report by the city's three senior officers produced the same day. If Labour made an illegal rate, there would be severe effects on the daily running of the council services. If the Government did not authorise borrowing, the city would not be able to pay its employees, its suppliers of goods and services, voluntary organisations or bond-holders. Suppliers would be reluctant to deal with the authority and investors and financial institutions reluctant to lend. The city might have to pay a high price in the future, as investors could force the authority to pay higher interest rates for its loans. 'Quite what the effect would be', the officials argued, 'it is impossible to say. There could be a gradual and protracted deterioration in services or a sudden and dramatic one, and there might be differences depending upon whether an insufficient rate was made or no rate at all.' But Tony Byrne's classic reply to all these legal strictures was, 'the morality of the stance we are taking over-rides what happens to be in the district auditor's report.' This view, that there was only one 'correct' position – their own – kept Labour going forward. And it unnerved many who had to deal with it.

Budget day – deadlock and on to the election

The party was not going to be diverted from its course. On 21 March the district Labour party reaffirmed its illegal strategy. The Labour group only had sight of the budget which might bankrupt them six days before the council meeting. Expenditure was planned at £m267, £m55 above the Government's target. The deficit budget was presented on 29 March after a march of 25,000 striking council workers and others, which had closed much of the city. The debate, which lasted over eight hours, was heated and controversial, with much discussion of class war and many accusations of treachery and retribution. But in the end, as expected, the six Labour rebels voted with the Conservatives and Liberals to defeat the deficit budget.

The real question was whether any alternative could be agreed. At one point the Government had been hoping that the Labour rebels could be persuaded to join a coalition of Liberals and Conservatives to produce a 'save the city' budget. And Patrick Jenkin had encouraged their leading spokesman, Paul Orr, to do so with an offer of 'More money than the city has ever seen from the Manpower Service Commission, the Sports

Council and the urban programme, if you get the show on the road with a legal budget.' But voting against illegality was one thing. Voting with the Liberals and Conservatives looked like treachery to the rebels, and they would not do it. Their reluctance was encouraged by the fact that the Liberals had already produced an alternative budget which was £m40 less than Labour's, but which they claimed would involve no cuts in jobs and services and a single figure rate rise. It was hardly a statesmanlike gesture at the height of the city's crisis. Even the Conservative party had ridiculed this as 'an unbankable sham' which was 'so irresponsible it would place us outside the law as surely as would the Labour party's declared intention.' In the time-honoured tradition of budgetary politics in Liverpool, the opposition parties failed to rise to the occasion. The pursuit of partisan self interest which had marked the lost decade still guided the behaviour of all parties on the council. Eventually, the meeting was abandoned without any budget agreed. It was not the first time it had happened in Liverpool. But this was quite different. A chasm of uncertainty had appeared.

National opinion was shocked by Liverpool's actions. The Labour leadership was especially appalled. John Cunningham argued 'I don't believe a Government can be blackmailed into giving extra resources by making a city bankrupt – it's the worst possible course of action to choose.' Accusing the Liverpool leadership of deliberately trying to mislead people about the city's finances, he argued there had been 'no proper working budget document in the city council chamber for many weeks and that's an unprecedented situation. And a number of people in senior positions in the group have decided to keep their cards close to their chest in the hope that this strategy and its implications would not be properly understood.' The Labour leadership was becoming infuriated by Liverpool's actions. But in a show of national elite solidarity in the face of provincial recalcitrance, Cunningham offered to lead a deputation of city councillors to Government Ministers to find a solution to the crisis. And Patrick Jenkin, while refusing to make a special case for Liverpool, replied 'My door is always open.' That offer, and its acceptance, in the end proved crucial. It opened the way to what the council had been after, and the Government had been resisting, real talks about Liverpool's financial problems.

In mid-April the two sides did meet again but failed to get any agreement. However two things did emerge which proved important later on. First, Jenkin promised that at some point he would visit the city. And in these talks, the idea first surfaced of holding an independent investigation of the previous ten years of the city's finances. Liverpool was pressing for this because they believed it would not only discredit the opposition parties, but would show that the crisis had not been invented by them, and had been developing during the last decade. But the Government did not want to get involved in that sort of investigation, and become more deeply immersed in Liverpool's financial problems, than was good for it. It offered instead an investigation by the district auditor of the city's services, in an effort to prove its own argument that Liverpool's financial troubles were caused by its own inefficiencies as much as by the Government's grant system. But even this was on offer only if Liverpool would first introduce a legal budget. The issue of an enquiry ran into the sand, along with all the other deliberations that were taking place, although the principle reappeared in a very important guise later on. But both sides were now waiting for the council elections in May and serious negotiations could not take place until then.

The Government was showing growing consternation at the obduracy of the Labour council and its willingness endlessly to repeat the simple argument that the Government had stolen its money and it wanted some of it back. After the meetings had broken down, Patrick Jenkin could scarcely credit what had happened and almost disbelievingly accused the Labour leaders of planning to commit 'municipal hari kari.' A former great city seemed on the point of collapse. A second budget meeting did take place on 25 April, but with the failure of the London talks to produce anything it was doomed from the start. The opposition parties had made no serious effort to get together to construct an alternative budget. And Labour was determined not to move.

The treasurer, Michael Reddington, described Labour's budget as 'frankly invalid.' But the Liberal proposals were so optimistic that Reddington described them as 'doubtfully realistic.' Both the opposition parties' budgets implied that the council could make annual savings at twice the rate ever achieved in the past. As throughout the lost decade, both were frightened by the electoral risks of putting forward the level of rate increase necessary to balance the books. Nobody could agree about anything and the meeting ended in disarray once more. The city was left without a budget in the second month of the financial year. Senior officials were left completely unsure of their legal right to spend or borrow money. The day after the meeting, the authority was virtually paralysed as they were frightened to buy even a postage stamp.

By May 1984, the Labour council's year long campaign had brought the city to the edge of a financial abyss. Nobody knew what lay ahead. The party certainly did not. The Government was amazed that things had gone so far. The national Labour leadership was embarrassed. Local officers were nervous and uncertain. The Church leaders were worried and leading the city in vigils of prayer. The only people who had not yet clearly spoken on the issue were the general public in Liverpool. So far, the whole affair had been dominated by political elites as they carried out their British Rail diplomacy between Liverpool and London. But now the voters would be given the chance to speak their mind and break the stalemate. The annual council elections were due on 5 May. The choice before the voters was an extraordinary one. But nobody really knew how the voters would react to Labour's threatened illegality and the dangers they had placed the city in. Would they solve the problem by throwing out the Militants and rejecting 'revolutionary defeatism?' Or did they believe that Labour had a case? And if so, would they vote for municipal bankruptcy? Their behaviour would be absolutely crucial for both sides.

LABOUR VINDICATED AND FIRST STEPS TO NEGOTIATION – The May 1984 Election

3

The May election was a crucial test of Labour's strategy and it became another turning point in the story. The result had a major effect upon the way Liverpool's case was treated by national elites. And it opened the way to genuine negotiations with a Government which until then had successfully managed to stay clear of the problem. One third of the 99 seats on the council were up for election in the thirty-three wards in the city. Obviously Labour had to win enough extra seats to make up for their six defectors and to get a majority for their deficit budget. But it also needed the voters' endorsement to strengthen its hand against the Government. Throughout the argument the Labour council had insisted that it had got not only union, but popular support, because of its council election victory in May 1983 on a platform of 'no cuts in jobs and services'. But its critics could legitimately argue that no one in 1983 knew they were voting for municipal bankruptcy. So the Liverpool Labour party badly wanted to get a 'double mandate' in 1984 for its illegal budget strategy. It knew this would increase enormously its ability to blackmail the Government into giving it some extra money. And it was confident it would win.

Labour ran an intensive campaign to persuade the voters to support them and it worked. Almost two months after the financial year 1984/85 had started, when Labour still had not made a budget and was threatening to take the city into the chaos of municipal bankruptcy, the party won the election and increased its majority by seven seats from 51 to 58. The Liberals and Conservatives combined got 41 seats. Even if the remaining five rebel Labour councillors voted with the opposition, the election had given Labour the majority to drive an illegal budget through the council.

In contrast to their national leadership, the local Labour party leaders immediately claimed the election had been a referendum on the budget crisis, which had produced a decisive result in favour of their illegality. In fact this was not entirely clear. Labour's success was to some extent a result of the types of seats being fought in the election. Labour was mainly defending safe seats in wards where it had won in the 1983 council election. By contrast the opposition parties were defending seats in vulnerable wards where they had lost in 1983. It would have been a major reversal of recent election trends in Liverpool if Labour had lost seats in 1984. Nevertheless, the election produced a massive 51 per cent turnout, 20 per cent up on 1983. And exactly as in 1983 Labour got 46 per cent of the votes, the highest in its history. In two years it had increased its seats on the Council by almost half. Whatever else, the threat of bankruptcy did not lose them support. The public mood in Liverpool continued to run very strongly in favour of the Labour party.

In fact, although Labour never had a majority on the city council between 1973 and 1983, the party had been gaining strength throughout the decade. Since its election disaster in 1973, when the Liberals first seized control of the new Liverpool city council after local government re-organisation, the Labour party had slowly been re-establishing its position. And despite the fact that it controlled the city for much of the decade, the Liberal party actually lost seats in all but one council election fought in Liverpool after their landslide victory in 1973, as table 1 in chapter 1 showed. That one very important exception was 1980. That was the controversial year in which the Labour council had raised the rates by 50 per cent to balance the books and it suffered the disaster of losing six seats, five of them to the Liberals. Prior to that election the Liberals were in decline and had lost almost forty per cent of their seats on the council in six years. That defeat after the large rate rise scarred the Labour party and affected its behaviour ever after.

But the key feature of that 1980 election was that, because the ward boundaries had been redrawn, all the council's 99 seats were being contested. And instead of one councillor in each ward standing for election, all three were fighting the seats. The effect was to increase dramatically the number of seats the Liberals won that year. Labour was likely to lose seats because of its rate rise. But instead of losing just one councillor in each ward, in some it actually lost all three. This was an enormous piece of electoral good fortune for the Liberal party which arrested their gradual decline and established them as a major force on the council once again. And it was the second time it had happened. In 1973, because of the reorganisation of local government, all the 99 seats had been contested which meant that Liberal votes again won them more seats on the council than would have been the case in a normal year if only one seat out of the three in every ward had been contested.

Labour had almost clawed itself back to equality from that setback in 1973 when it lost badly again in 1980. And it had been regaining ground since then. The long term voting trend in Liverpool was very much against the Liberals in favour of the Labour party, which again increased the likelihood of a Labour victory in the 1984 election. The same was true of parliamentary elections. Labour made gains throughout the decade, but this time at the expense of the Conservatives. In the 1983 general election, held six weeks after the council elections which had given Labour its first majority for a decade, the Conservative Party finally lost its one remaining MP in the city. Nationally, the general election results showed a swing from Labour to Conservative of 3.9 per cent. But in Liverpool the swing was 2.4 per cent away from the Conservatives to Labour. The Liverpool Labour party would needed to have done very badly to have lost the 1984 council elections.

Nevertheless, the Labour council was naturally jubilant with the results and its victory. Government officials knew the long-term voting trends, and were not completely surprised. But they still found it hard to understand why so many people had voted for a party apparently intent on financial suicide. Some answers to this crucial question were provided by our survey of over 1,200 voters conducted by National Opinion Polling in Liverpool during the week after the election. The survey explored peoples' understanding of the crisis, their motives and expectations, their hopes and their fears. It told us how much they knew about the crisis, what they expected the Labour council and the Government to do as well as what they wanted them to do. The poll provided a very clear insight into the mood of the city, in particular the widespread frustration about its decline, and possible reaction if the Conservative Government tried to impose draconian solutions from outside. It helped explain why the Conservatives had finally lost support in the city during the last five years, and a hard left Labour party had emerged to take control of the council. And it also suggested why the Conservative Government does not like Liverpool and has grown tired of its 'special pleading.'

Opinion poll

Despite Labour's elaborate year-long campaign, as might have been expected in these complicated areas, very few people actually understood many of the central issues of the budget drama. For example, there was enormous confusion in voters' minds about what Labour would do if it was re-elected. The majority of even Labour voters, in fact, thought the party would back down from its illegal stance if it won. There was equal uncertainty about what the Government would do if Labour did not back down – whether it would impose commissioners, leave things to the courts, make severe cuts in Liverpool services or make financial concessions itself to the city. In fact, fewest people thought the Government would make any concessions. In other words, when they voted the majority were confused and fearing the worst outcome. Of course the voters were not on their own in this respect. Throughout the crisis, even those most intimately involved had no idea how the issue would finally be settled. The endless manoeuvrings and efforts to read the entrails to discover the other side's real intentions were a constant feature of the confrontation. Nevertheless, despite their worries and confusion many of the electorate still supported Labour.

But the election was not really, as Labour claimed, a direct referendum upon the merits of municipal bankruptcy. In fact, very few people voted specifically in those terms. The majority of Labour and Conservative voters actually voted out of traditional loyalty to their party. The campaign particularly strengthened Labour voters support for their party, without necessarily convincing them of its plan for an illegal budget. The real importance of the confrontation with the Government was not to provide understanding or persuade people on the detailed arguments, but to strengthen the voters' existing party loyalties. For example, when asked who was responsible for the crisis, the large majority of people in all three parties blamed the other side for the crisis. Very few were willing to share the blame amongst all those who had actually been involved locally and nationally, and had contributed to the crisis, during the previous decade.

Similarly, few voters were willing to believe what the other parties said about the city's financial problems. For example, the Labour council had claimed it needed a rate rise of 170 per cent to balance the books. The other parties had said a rise of less than 30 per cent would do. But only about 10 per cent of Labour and Liberal voters and less than 5 per cent of Conservatives believed the other parties were telling the truth. Labour's tactic of dramatising the issue and only presenting stark alternatives, had the desired effect. It may have driven away Liberal and Conservative voters, but it made sure that its own traditional supporters believed their case. Given the importance to Labour of getting a high turnout and making sure their working-class supporters voted, its campaign succeeded.

Local chauvinism and protest

But if the pattern of public opinion did not confirm Labour's more extravagant claims about the election, there was nevertheless a very strong current of public support for Labour's challenge to the Government and in particular a very strong sense of grievance about the Conservative's treatment of the city. In fact the most marked feature of opinion was a strand of local chauvinism which ran through all three political parties. The voters were protesting to the Government. More ominously, they were warning it that protest could turn to resistance if the Government attempted to take control of the city and put Liverpool's house in order.

Voters were asked, for example, which forms of opposition to central government commissioners they would support: public demonstrations, occupation of the council offices by local authority workers who had been made redundant; non-cooperation by council workers with the commissioners; strikes by council workers; rent and rate strikes and a general strike by all workers. And the survey, to which both the Government and the Labour councillors paid close attention, provided little hope that the commissioners' occupation of the city could be a quiet one.

Opinion was polarised along party lines as table 1 shows. But an important strand of anti-Government and pro-Liverpool, as opposed to pro-Labour party, thought emerged. The Conservative voters in the city opposed resistance, especially since it would be directed against their own party in Government. But Liberal voters were more mixed. Although they blamed the Labour council and the Government for the crisis, substantial minorities of Liberals consistently approved of all forms of opposition to the commissioners. Particularly significant, 28

Table 1: Opposing a Central Government Take-over

	Labour			Liberal			Conservative		
By means of:	approve	disapprove	not sure	approve	disapprove	not sure	approve	disapprove	not sure
		%			%			%	
Demonstrations	62	31	6	17	79	3	8	87	5
Occupation by redundant council workers	68	25	7	28	64	8	8	83	8
Strike by council workers	59	32	9	14	80	6	4	91	5
General strike	55	34	11	14	77	8	5	87	8
Council workers refusing to cooperate with commissioners	56	32	4	14	77	8	2	89	9
Rent and rates strike	48	41	11	22	71	7	8	85	8

per cent would approve of resistance by any local authority workers who were made redundant by the commissioners. Jobs, and public sector jobs, were an emotive theme even for Labour's opponents.

But support for resistance was inevitably strongest amongst the Labour supporters. As with the Liberals the prospect of unemployment was again the most important issue, reflecting public worries in a city with 60,000 people out of work. Almost 70 per cent of Labour voters were in favour of the occupation of council offices by local authority workers if they were made redundant. Large numbers of Labour supporters also favoured the more extreme forms of resistance. Almost half were in favour of rent and rate strikes. And 55 per cent of Labour voters would support a general strike. If attitudes were a reliable guide to future behaviour, the Government could expect trouble. At best the administration of the city's services would be problematic. At worst, there could be sustained political confrontation between the commissioners and the public, and the possibility of guerilla like violence.

Of course, the Government had contingency plans for commissioners, even though there was a lot of uncertainty about which kinds of people would be willing and able to serve. For example, it was felt that former local authority officials might not be sufficiently hardline to enforce the cuts in jobs and services that might be necessary. Someone from private industry might be tough enough but might also be too controversial. Former civil servants might not have the necessary experience or capacity to carry local officials with them. Some believed that someone with experience in public sector trade unions would be necessary to persuade the workforce to cooperate.

Spotting the commissioners became something of a local, even a national, pastime. There was no shortage of volunteers. The Government received many unsolicited offers from people without any qualifications for the job, except an intense desire to sort out Liverpool and the Militant Tendency. But such delicate concerns about personnel paled into insignificance in comparison with the problems the Government knew might face the commissioners trying to run the city. The problems experienced by commissioners in Clay Cross in 1972, who had a much narrower role in a much less politically volatile place, was hardly encouraging. Their first problem would be in getting the doors of the offices unlocked and then finding a working telephone. Indeed the standing joke in Government circles was that since they would never get off the end of the local motorway, the commissioners would need offices with a flat roof to allow the helicopters taking them in and out of the city to land. The question was how far, and in what form, opposition might develop and what the political consequences might be for the Government. However successful its occupation of the city, it could be no more than an exercise in damage limitation with few tangible political benefits.

The explanation of the extraordinary public willingness to resist the Government lay in the depth of the pro-city, anti-Government sentiment which ran through voters in all the political parties. The Government claimed, for example, that Liverpool was not only treated fairly and equally by the grant system, but that it had also received a whole battery of special programmes and initiatives in recent years which meant that in some respects Liverpool had done even better than other cities. Labour argued, by contrast, that the Government was punishing the city financially and that its special initiatives nowhere near compensated for the £m 270 that the Conservatives had 'stolen' from the city.

Not surprisingly, virtually all Labour voters believed the council. But even amongst Liberal voters who blamed the Labour group for the immediate crisis, only one third believed the Government's argument. The majority of Liberals actually believed Labour. Even among Conservatives, who in almost every other respect took the Government's side, a substantial minority believed Labour's claim that Liverpool had had a raw deal from the Government. And even though few people believed it would do so, almost three quarters of Labour voters, two thirds of Liberals and half of even Conservatives, wanted the Government to make a special case and find some extra money to help the city through the immediate crisis. When it saw the results of the poll, the Government rightly concluded it was not getting its message across to substantial proportions of its own supporters, let alone the opposition parties in Liverpool.

The local chauvinism extended across the parties to their views about the long-term future of Liverpool. For example, people indicated which they thought was the most realistic view of the city's future: that Liverpool was bound to decline and little could be done to help it; that its problems could be resolved if the Government would introduce new programmes and increase public spending; or that the city's problems

Table 2: Has Liverpool Had a Fair Deal?

	Labour	Liberal	Conservative
		%	
Not fair	89	53	28
Fair	5	33	61
Not sure	6	14	11

could be solved if all the local institutions and groups could work together more successfully. Perhaps the most extraordinary feature of the responses was the general optimism about the city's long term future that pervaded all parties. Although Labour voters tended to place more emphasis on Government spending than the others, all parties believed that many of the city's problems were in fact soluble by local action. In many respects this was an unrealistic view of the city's future. But it gives some indication of the extent of patriotism in the beleaguered city which lay at the root of the pervasive resentment of the Government's apparent lack of concern for the city. One voter canvassed by a Liberal candidate expressed the mood precisely in saying 'I can't stand the Militant. But at least someone is standing up to the Bitch in London.'

Table 3: How Could Liverpool be Saved?

	Labour	Liberal	Conservative
		%	
Public spending	38	17	11
Local actions	35	60	63
Bound to decline	17	15	17
Not sure	11	10	10

Support for a deficit budget?

But support for Labour was as much a gesture of defiance at the Government as it was an endorsement of bankruptcy. It drew upon a deep well of anti-Thatcherism in the city. This was clear from voters view of what Labour should do if it was re-elected. Despite their residual resentment of the Government and their hopes for special treatment, Conservative and Liberal voters were completely opposed to illegality. This was to be expected. But, the majority of Labour voters were also opposed to Labour's plans for illegality. 46 per cent of those who actually voted for Labour did not want a deficit budget; 18 per cent had still not made up their mind even after they had voted. Only 35 per cent of people who voted Labour wanted the council to default.

In other words, a minority of Labour supporters – a fifth of all voters in the city – agreed with the Labour council that the city's financial problems were so great that they might as well stage the final confrontation with the Government and plunge the city into bankruptcy. Frustration at and resentment of Thatcherism had apparently driven most people to vote Labour rather than an active endorsement of bankruptcy. But the problem was that despite their qualifications, the voters actually encouraged the Labour party to go along that road. The vote could not capture the ambiguity of people's feelings. If Labour wanted to claim a decisive victory, it would also have to claim a decisive mandate for bankruptcy as well.

But while a minority of even Labour voters, 35 per cent was still a large number of people in favour of such an extreme course. Who were they? Our survey showed that they were not predominantly council house tenants, but they were just as likely as other Labour voters to own their own homes. They were certainly no more likely to be unemployed. They were in general a little younger than the moderate Labour supporters. They were certainly not drawn from the least well-off sections of the city. In fact they were rather more likely to be in professional, middle class jobs, and less likely to be in manual, working class jobs than other Labour voters. In other words, the Labour 'resisters', as we call them, were not typically the older, poorer, unemployed, council tenants who were economically displaced, with little to lose from an act of despair. It was rather the other way round. They were more likely to be younger, working, professional and middle-class property owners – the new hard Left.

In fact it was the ideological differences between Labour voters which revealed most about their attitude to the crisis. Labour voters divided into one-third hard Left who identified with Tony Benn, and two-thirds soft Left who identified with Neil Kinnock. The two sets of supporters were remarkably alike in terms of their class background. But they had quite different political views about Liverpool's financial problem. Kinnock supporters were considerably more moderate. A majority in both camps supported virtually all kinds of resistance to the commissioners. But Benn supporters were much stronger in their opposition. In fact, Kinnock's supporters drew the line at rent and rate strikes to which a small majority were actually opposed, whereas the majority of Benn voters were in favour of such a strike. However, the difference was clearest in their attitude to the illegal budget. Kinnock supporters were far less willing to go bankrupt. 65 per cent were opposed to it, and only 35 per cent were in favour. But in the case of Benn supporters, the position was reversed – 35 per cent opposed illegality but 65 per cent were in favour.

As many as 51 per cent of the electorate turned out to vote – an extraordinarily high figure for a local election. And the confrontation appeared to touch everyone in the city and involved them equally. Women voted as often as men. The social classes behaved similarly, with working class people voting only a little less frequently than middle and upper middle class groups. The highest turnout came from housewives and old age pensioners. But the unemployed, for example, voted almost as heavily as the employed. Nor did housing tenure affect turnout. Identical proportions of home-owners, council tenants and private renters voted. Whatever their views about the causes of the problem, the people in Liverpool were obviously affected and mobilised by it.

The council workers

But the most distinctive group of voters were the 30,000 local authority workers. They were by far the largest group of employees in either the public or private sector in the city. And they were most immediately involved in and affected by the illegal budget and possible cuts in services or jobs. The issues mobilised them. Council workers turned out in massive numbers with 80 per cent of all groups – teachers, social workers, blue collar workers and white collar administrators – voting. And the issues also radicalised them. Other workers voted 13 per cent Conservative, 30 per cent Liberal and 55 per cent Labour. But council employees voted 11 per cent Conservative, 15 per cent Liberal and a massive 72 per cent Labour. A decade of Liberal control had lost them support amongst the workforce. All the council workers who had been mobilised by the confrontation and who, for example, voted in 1984 but had not voted in 1983, supported Labour. By contrast, the non-council workers who had voted in 1984 but not 1983 were marginally more in favour of the Liberals.

The radicalisation of council workers was also demonstrated by their much greater willingness than the rest of workers in Liverpool to oppose the Government's commissioners. They were far more willing to take part in demonstrations and sit-ins, to support strikes by council workers, or a general strike, as well as rents and rate strikes. And they were willing by a much larger margin to support strikes by council workers if they were made redundant. However, despite their support for the Labour party, the council workers were no more anxious to see an illegal budget than the rest of the city's voters. Only 25 per cent of council workers, as opposed to 20 per cent of all voters, favoured the illegal budget. Their greater militancy stopped at this. To some extent, self-interest drove the council workers along this path. But it was still true that the group whose interests were most directly entwined with the issues in the dispute, had been most exposed to the full thrust of Labour's propaganda campaign and had most direct experience of the impact of their predecessor's policies, were far more in support of the Labour council than any other group of voters in the city.

The Government could never really understand why the workforce supported Labour in its stand. They thought it was irrational since it would lead to chaos and the eventual loss of more jobs than if Labour compromised. There were two union responses to this. The first was that if the Government and its commissioners would have to sack local authority workers in the end, there was no reason for the Labour council to anticipate that and do the Government's dirty work. The unions would rather fight the Tories about the cuts than the Labour council. Also there was some feeling that the commissioners might be reluctant to sack people and that the Government would bail them out with some extra money. In which case, the cuts might not be too bad. The second response was that if the Labour council did raise the rates by the figure necessary to balance the books, it would be tantamount to losing the next election and turning control of the city back to the Liberals. At which point, the unions believed that their job would be threatened by a combination of privatisation and natural wastage under a Liberal administration. Either way, the unions calculated the best thing to do was to stay behind the Labour council.

This radicalisation of the workforce had serious implications for a Government contemplating taking over Liverpool. Any attempt by commissioners to balance the budget quickly might need large staff cuts. Given workforce attitudes, this could be politically dangerous for the Government. It realised that if commissioners could not make the necessary savings in the short term, their period of office might run to several years before the city's services and workforce could be reduced sufficiently to meet Government spending limits, at a pace the workforce would tolerate. It also knew that the city's politicians during the lost decade of the 1970s had failed to deal with many of the problems of the blue-collar workforce because of political and administrative pressures. The Government would be in the difficult position of similarly trying to rationalise those sectors to achieve its economies while faced with the exteme hostility of all city workers. And it might have to stay in Liverpool far longer than might be good for it. The survey, like the electorate itself, made bleak reading for the Government and confirmed their worst fears about their standing in Liverpool. And it heightened their dilemma.

The lessons of the election

The question the Government asked itself after the May election was why people had voted in such large numbers for the Labour party and financial suicide. It seemed self-destructive. The answer was that they were actually protesting to the Government. The extent of popular discontent in Liverpool was in fact even greater than the election results suggested. Many more than Labour voters were opposed to Government policies, and even some of their own supporters had doubts. Not surprisingly, popular understanding of the technical budget issues was slight and people seemed confused about what was going to happen. But these are difficult matters which have defeated the initiated including, occasionally, Patrick Jenkin himself.

But the voters had grasped the main outlines of the story and connected it with the picture of obvious economic,physical and social decline they could witness daily around them. The private sector was collapsing and unemployment was rising and lasting longer. However tangentially related, crime and drug abuse was also seen to be on the increase. Under these circumstances, the Government's policy of cutting public expenditure and reducing the money spent on housing and local authority jobs, seemed to lack commonsense. The budget stood at the intersection of all these issues. Very few people wanted the council to break the law. But in their frustration, many wanted Labour to take the struggle to the Government in some kind of act of collective defiance. Symbolically, the election almost seemed like Liverpool's last stand. And it had a dramatic effect on the outcome of the confrontation in 1984.

Labour's May election victory transformed the politics of the budget struggle in 1984. The position had become very different for both sides. Labour's threats and the dangers to themselves and the city were more realistic. The Government's faint hope that the electorate would be frightened off by Labour's stand had disappeared. They could no longer claim that the electorate did not know the implications of voting Labour as it had been able to argue about the 1983 election. Both had to consider how to play the confrontation and how much they were willing to compromise to avoid the chaos of bankruptcy.

Labour saw no need to compromise. The election results had strengthened their hand enormously. They had received the so-called double mandate from the people of Liverpool, they believed that right was now clearly on their side and they could press the Government still further. Derek Hatton insisted 'this must be a warning to Jenkin that he is not just taking on 58 Labour councillors. The people have spoken very loudly and clearly in favour of the policies of the Liverpool Labour party tonight. And it is a warning Mr. Jenkin must take notice of.' None of the Labour group knew what would happen next. Many were nervous and worried about their own future. But, ironically, all of them became further committed to the policy by their election success. Both the councillors whose personal futures were at stake, and the district Labour party whose generally were not, believed that Labour would seem foolish and damage its reputation in the city, if it retreated from illegality in the aftermath of its victory.

The Government's dilemma

But the Government was even more trapped by the results. Uncertainty was still very high and it could not be sure which way the workforce would move as the risk of municipal collapse loomed. But the voters had made their views clear. And the Government did not know whether the new Labour majority on the council would disintegrate. But all the new Labour councillors had known what they were getting into and were, in fact, less likely than any existing councillors to defect in future. If Labour now pressed on and the Government did nothing, it might lose control of events with unpredictable political consequences for itself. If it installed commissioners, the prospect of running the city on a very tight budget was equally alarming. But, if it made concessions to Liverpool it would reinforce doubts about its current grant system. Most important, it would be seen giving in to blackmail and anger other Labour cities and Conservative counties who were trying to cope with different degrees of financial difficulties. Anything it might do was bound to be taken as a precedent for future years by other local authorities. All its options had drawbacks.

But after Labour's election victory the odds shifted in favour of the Government making short term concessions to Labour, extricating itself from the conflict and trying to limit the political damage, rather than becoming increasingly embroiled in a battle which it did not want and felt might not be won. The Government's immediate reaction in the new war of nerves was a hardline one. Replying to Liverpool MPs claims, Jenkin argued that there could be no electoral mandate for an illegal act. And there was 'no question of our even contemplating putting in commissioners until the situation has dramatically broken down in Liverpool, until the local council has absolutely shown beyond a per-adventure that they are not prepared to keep services going, they are not prepared to do what is necessary for the city to remain within the law.' It was very important for the Government that if it did take over the city, it did so only after everyone understood that the Liverpool Labour party had recklessly brought the chaos to the city. In that way, the Conservatives would appear like the saviour of a city on its knees, rather than an avenging monetarist regime trying to strangle at birth a popular socialist administration. So for the time being, Liverpool was to be left to stew in its own juices.

But, elsewhere the mood was changing as a result of the election. The people had apparently spoken and everyone was now anxious to line up behind them. The local press, while still critical of Labour's course, began to emphasise the need for Government flexibility. The Roman Catholic Archbishop, Derek Worlock, while criticising extremism asked 'is it really out of the question that discussion and even negotiation should take place?' More important, the national Labour Party line was changing. It could see an opportunity to break the stalemate without too much electoral damage to itself, by using the council's popularity against the Thatcher Government. Although Kinnock was still pressing Liverpool to fix a legal rate, his response to their victory was that 'it now would really make a lot of sense for Patrick Jenkin to find some extra money for the city.' And John Cunningham soon offered to mediate between the two sides, arguing there now was 'a clear and broad consensus in favour of a settlement of the city's problem which goes right across the churches, voluntary bodies as well as across the political parties.' The issue should be resolved by negotiations between the two sides 'not by allowing the problems of the city to slide into chaos.'

The Negotiations

Labour's election victory made it difficult for the Government to resist this line. It had shown that, whatever the immediate details of the financial crisis, many people believed at least some of Labour's argument that the Government was not treating fairly a city with severe economic problems. The pressures upon the Government to now enter into negotiations were growing. It did not want them because it could see the political risks involved. It would open up the whole question of its grant system and could start raising doubts about it. But it was even harder to refuse.

In the end the opportunity to turn the general wish for further negotiations into reality was quite fortuitous. On a previous visit to Liverpool to see the International Garden Festival, Patrick Jenkin had refused to meet the Labour council's demand that he inspect derelict housing instead. But he said he would do so in the future.

A routine enquiry from the press in early May to find out when the Minister would be coming to the city led his unwitting private office in Liverpool to reveal the arranged date was 7 June. This public announcement allowed the delighted Labour leaders to claim that Jenkin had been persuaded after all to come and see Liverpool's financial problems at first hand. The appalled Minister was forced to deny this interpretation the following day in Parliament. He insisted he was going to Liverpool to look at housing problems as a background to future housing capital allocations. The visit had 'no connection with the council's budget-making and rate-fixing process and there must be no misunderstanding about that.'

But it was too late. The district Labour party had postponed the planned council budget meeting on 15 May until after Jenkin's visit. The Liverpool MPs in Parliament were welcoming his initiative, applauding the constructive move by Liverpool's leaders, and asking Patrick Jenkin to go without 'rigid, preconceived ideas.' The Labour leaders now believed that it would be very difficult for the Minister, after such a long publicised visit, to dash expectations and make no constructive response, particularly as sympathy for the city's financial predicament seemed to be growing. Labour had gained an important political advantage over the Government.

John Cunningham now stepped in on behalf of the national Labour Party and set up a further round of talks between Liverpool and the Government. And from these talks in May between councillors, MPs, trade union officials, civil servants and Ministers, a very important initiative emerged. Both sides agreed that a joint team of senior civil servants and local authority officials would begin a series of discussions, without politicians present, to explore the financial arguments and try to construct alternative proposals which might form the basis of a new budget before the Minister's visit on 7 June. The idea had first been discussed in the meetings between the two sides in London in April. But at that time Labour had wanted an enquiry into the last ten years of the city's financial affairs, while the Government had wanted the district auditor to do an expose of Liverpool's services. These discussions were neither of those two. But the 'joint report' which they produced played a key role in producing the eventual settlement in July 1984.

The talks were intensive lasting over three weeks in May and June and involved frequent visits to Liverpool by a team of senior Departmental officials, including Terry Heiser, the man who had invented the grant system and who was soon to be made Permanent Secretary of the Department of the Environment. There were extensive negotiations between the London civil servants, members of the Task Force and senior council officials. The process was closely monitored on a weekly basis in London by the most senior Ministers – the Prime Minister herself, Patrick Jenkin, Michael Heseltine, Norman Tebbitt, Leon Brittan and Tom King. The negotiations in effect suspended political debate about Liverpool's budget. When the 'joint report' was finally produced, as well as a set of proposals for resolving the immediate budgetary crisis, it contained a fascinating detailed discussion of both sides' views of the long term causes of the city's financial problems.

The discussions were crucial to the course of the confrontation. In the first place they allowed detailed discussions to take place in which changes of positions could occur and which helped identify the basis of a settlement in 1984. Before then there had never been any genuine negotiations in meetings between the two sides, at either a political or an official level. Both had rehearsed their familiar lines, essentially talking past each other. This was probably intentional. The Government only wanted to tell Liverpool to obey the law like everyone else – not to get drawn into an argument about the origins or scale of the city's problems. Also they simply did not trust the Labour leadership. The Labour leaders, for their part, did not want to abandon their ultimate sanction – the threat of plunging the city into bankruptcy – until they were quite certain that the Government was not willing to make concessions which would give Liverpool an ideological as well as a financial victory.

The second important political result of the negotiations were that they demonstrated that, whatever their scale, the city's financial problems were real. Nothing conveyed the political implications of the 'joint report' more vividly than the banner headline of the Liverpool Echo on the day it was leaked – 'Whitehall Whiz Kids Stumped.' Despite the protestations of civil servants, the Labour party concluded that its own position had been strengthened, and the Government's undermined, by the negotiations and that they represented a major propaganda victory for Liverpool.

This was allied in Labour's view to that scored one week later when

Patrick Jenkin made his long-awaited and much publicised tour of the city's housing, which had a curious parallel to Michael Heseltine's tour of the riot zone of Toxteth three years earlier. After the tour, Jenkin announced, 'I have seen some families living in conditions the like of which I have never seen before. They are very grim.' Whether the Secretary of the Environment should not have seen such housing before, whether it was actually worse in Liverpool than anywhere else, or whether he should have admitted it publicly, are all open questions. But his admission was a major tactical error and only reinforced the fact that Patrick Jenkin could now hardly avoid making some offer on housing to the city, without severe political embarrassment. When it was announced that talks would take place about ways of giving Liverpool extra housing aid, it looked like the Government was also trying to find money to help the council balance its books. And this is exactly what the Liverpool Labour leaders claimed. They had set up the Government for a fall and were now waiting to push it over.

The May 1984 election had been crucial for both sides. And the Liverpool Labour party successfully used its victory to outmanoeuvre the Government. The victory brought many people over to its side and gave its argument a new legitimacy. It could no longer be argued that the council had hijacked the city. It had popular support. The Government found it could no longer maintain its distance from the problem. Instead, it got publicly drawn much deeper into Liverpool's financial problems than it wanted and was forced to admit that they were real and urgent. It could now hardly refuse to make some initiative without appearing unreasonable to an outside world which was showing increasing sympathy with Liverpool's case and looking for a negotiated settlement. And much of this had been achieved by the negotiations between the two sets of professionals in May and June and their final 'joint report.' But what did it show about their political masters' claims? Had the Labour council invented the financial crisis merely to launch an attack on the Conservative Government? Had the voters of Liverpool been duped by the Militant Tendency? Was the Government right that the city's problems were quite manageable given common sense and political will? Or did Liverpool have a case that the Government's policy had created for it an impossible financial situation?

LIVERPOOL AGAINST WHITEHALL: THE PROFESSIONALS JOIN IN – May - June 1984

4

If Labour's election victory was one decisive turning point in the budget saga, the negotiations between civil servants and local officials, and their final 'joint report', were another. They created a space for political manoeuvring and led to the eventual settlement. But they were also a serious attempt to look at the longer-term financial issues which underpinned Liverpool's ideological challenge to the Government. And the negotiations revealed that, whatever they thought about the way the Labour party presented its argument politically, Liverpool's professional officers also believed that the city had a good case and the Government was in the wrong. Labour had not invented the problem even if it was exploiting it.

In the officers' eyes, the Government's grant system, and the assumptions underlying it, punished Liverpool in an arbitrary and unacceptable way. The system lacked a sense of proportion about the city's financial and economic problems and made a bad situation worse. Michael Reddington, the city treasurer, likened it to being on the side of an icy mountain – the further you slid down, the harder it was to stop the slide and rescue yourself, even if you were trying. It might have needed Thatcher, Hatton and Byrne to start the political fight. But in the officers' minds, the reasons for it had been lurking around for some time. The civil servants, like their Ministers, could not have disagreed more. The size of the gap between the two became crystal clear during the negotiations in May 1984.

The Government's grant system – giving and taking money

The Labour party's argument with the Government was essentially a political one based on its rejection of Thatcherite economic policies and their impact upon a declining city like Liverpool. But it rested on a technical critique of the way the Government allocated money to the city, which tied into the larger argument about the labrynthine rate support grant the Conservatives developed in the 1980s. The political argument was about values, mandates and the rule of law. The technical argument was about administrative and financial rationality and was developed by the city's professional officers.

There are two kinds of local spending – capital and revenue. Capital expenditure buys buildings, land and plant which have a long-term life, and is paid for primarily by long-term borrowing. Revenue expenditure is mainly the annual cost of providing services like education, housing, social services, leisure and cultural facilities, transport and cleansing. Over half of revenue spending covers employees' wages and salaries, one third running costs and the rest covers debt charges. About half of the money is received from Government grant, one third from the rates and the rest from rents and fees. About 85 per cent of Government grant comes as a general block grant and the rest for specific services like housing, transport, the police and the urban programme. Most of the recent political controversy has been about the way the block grant system works. It was the basic cause of Liverpool's argument with the Thatcher Government which tried to use the system to cut the financial support it gave local authorities, as well as to cut what they spent from their own income.

The block grant system is extremely complicated and has changed several times since it was first introduced by the Conservative Government in 1981. But in principle it attempts to do two rather different things. On the one hand it tries to use central government money to equalise the financial position of local authorities and to make sure that local authorities with very different financial resources can provide a similar level of local service which their different populations need, for a similar rate level.

But at the same time the grant system is also meant to reduce local government spending by penalising individual authorities who spend more than the Government tells them to. The first is a relatively systematic, if complicated, way of allocating Government money to local authorities. The second is a much more arbitrary way of reducing local expenditure, which undermines the first intention of equalising the financial circumstances of different authorities. And as the Conservative Government has tried harder through the 1980s to limit the spending of

Labour-controlled local authorities, the second has become harsher and more controversial.

Every year the Government decides the total amount of money it wants local authorities to spend the following year, and what percentage of that local spending it will pay for. Both have been cut back in recent years. Between 1979/80 and 1985/86, the percentage of local expenditure the Conservative Government paid for fell drastically, from 61 per cent to 48 per cent. And between 1981/82 and 1985/86 the total block grant fell in real terms by 16 per cent. This forced up rate levels to provide the same level of local services.

Once the total block grant has been decided, it is distributed between individual local authorities in an extremely complicated way, which has created enormous conflict. Through a complex series of over sixty different kinds of computer based analyses, in which a whole range of indicators of local need are identified, quantified and given different weightings, the Government calculates what it thinks an authority should spend, given the social, economic, environmental and geographical composition of its population. This is called its grant-related expenditure assessment. The Government then calculates how much income a local authority would raise with a particular rate level, given the rateable value of the property in its area. The difference between that figure and the total the Government has determined the authority needs to spend, is what the authority gets as its block grant from the Government. In this way, ratepayers can expect to receive the same standard of service for the same rate in the pound, wherever they live and no matter how rich or how poor their local authority is. But much of this depends on whether the Government's assessment of what an authority needs to spend is accurate and fair. Liverpool has consistently disagreed with the Government about this.

However complicated the process of deciding an authority's needs and the grant it should get, it is at least systematic. But this is not true of the target and penalty system which the Government simply grafted on to the block grant system in 1982, in order to tighten its control over local authority spending. Since then the Government every year has set each local authority an expenditure target figure, and if the authority spends above it, it has to pay a penalty – the Government cuts the amount of grant it had originally calculated the authority should get. The authority has to increase its rates to compensate for the Government's cut in grant, if it wants to keep up its spending.

The way in which targets and penalties are calculated is again very complicated and has changed several times since they were first introduced. The original targets for 1981/82 were determined simply by taking each local authority's spending in 1978/79 and cutting it by 5.6 per cent in real terms. The base years for calculating targets have since changed, and the Government's assessment of local need also plays a part in determining them. But the principle, that its previous expenditure levels broadly determine an authority's target, remains. Local authorities have simply been asked systematically to cut back spending from earlier levels. Whereas the Government's assessment of need is a relatively objective measure for allocating grant, local expenditure in a single year can be determined by many things, and might bear no real relationship to need. It is not a similarly objective method of deciding what grant an authority should get.

The penalties for overspending target have become progressively tougher and now increase very steeply. The more an authority spends, the higher the penalty it pays. For example, in 1984/85 if an authority spent 1 per cent over its target, it would have to increase its rate by 2p to compensate for its loss of Government grant. If it spent 6 per cent over its target, it would have to increase its rates by 41p to cover for the cut in grant. Once again, rate payers pay a heavy price for keeping services at a spending level beyond the Government's target figure. This has caused intense political controversy, not only in high-spending Labour but in many low-spending Conservative authorities, which the target system has also penalised. And it has raised technical questions of whether the target system is not simply too primitive a way of deciding how much Government support an authority should get. Even the Government's own quango on local government finance, the Audit Commission, for example, in 1984 argued that the grant system, with its needs assessment and equalisation machinery was broadly fair and consistent. But it had been significantly weakened by the superimposition of expenditure targets and penalties.

In the mid-1980s the Government was still unhappy about its failure to control local spending as many local authorities refused to cut their spending down to Government targets, and increased their rates to make up for the loss of Government grant. In 1985 the Minister, with his rate-capping legislation, actually took the power to control local spending by determining what rate levels the highest spending local authorities could set. By this time a system which had set out to rationalise local government spending was under constant attack from virtually all quarters. It was seen by many independent observers as a complicated, irrational and arbitrary system, which at best had seriously damaged local democracy and relations between central and local government. The left regarded it as a punitive attack by a sectarian, monetarist Government on the social wage of an urban working class already suffering badly from Conservative policies.

Professional tensions

Liverpool's dispute with the Government revolved around many of the technical issues raised by this new grant system – the way the Government calculated grant entitlement, its use of targets and penalties, the way the city managed and financed its services, the implications of rapid social and demographic change for public sector organisations. Liverpool's officials' essential argument was that the city's problems were primarily caused by the damaging effect of the Government's grant regime upon its finances, and that everything else was relatively trivial in significance. In their view, the system was irrational, providing no incentives for prudential accounting behaviour and punishing the local authority very heavily for minor breaches of the rules. The system was so severe that it made it difficult to get a rational political response to it. Especially in a period of economic decline, the system itself was fundamentally destabilising. In city treasurer Michael Reddington's words, 'There used to be a spirit to the game, but the rules have been changed. The Government keeps moving the goalposts.' The view of Departmental officials, however, was that its grant system was reasonable and equitable. It did not discriminate against Liverpool. The city's problems were of its own making and the remedy was in its own hands. It was badly managed, overstaffed, inefficient and expensive.

These professional arguments were fully developed in the joint discussions between civil servants and local officials in May 1984. There was a particular piquancy to the negotiations because they directly involved the man who had designed the grant system, Terry Heiser, a rising star who was subsequently appointed Permanent Secretary, in a flurry of publicity, at the age of 53. In other words, they brought face-to-face, in a quite unique way, the authors of the system with the officers who were grappling with the problems of implementing it in a hard-pressed local authority. Liverpool's officials could not help feeling that the civil servants' tenacity in defence of the grant system was affected by this fact. In one official's words, civil servants were having to 'defend the indefensible', and it was not clear to him 'whether they actually believe in what they are doing or just say they do.' The civil servants had the tiger by the tail and it was threatening to turn on them. But at the end of it all a senior civil servant responded 'I don't know anybody in Whitehall who believes Liverpool's claims about the problem of the grant regime.' Both sets of officials not only presented the arguments of their political masters. They believed them as well.

The negotiations touched many of the raw nerves that characterise relations between the professionals in central and local government. In many respects 'a culture of disdain' exemplifies the attitudes of senior civil servants towards the local authority world. The mandarins' sense of elite superiority frequently leads them to undervalue local government officials. They in turn are often frustrated by the fact that civil servants set the rules from on high, but never have to put them into practice. The extent of this cultural gap was made very clear by the joint discussions. Civil servants became increasingly intolerant of Liverpool officials' arguments, which they regarded as special pleading. Local officials were disenchanted by the civil servants' attempt to apply standards to the local authority which their own Departments would never meet, as well as by their refusal to admit the unreasonableness of the grant system, which Liverpool's officials called 'wayward and capricious'. If the politicians talked past each other during the argument, in many ways the professionals did as well.

Despite these professional tensions, however, the 'joint report' they produced was not a narrowly argued analysis, and it remains the authoritative statement of Liverpool's budgetary problems. For political reasons, the Liverpool Labour party always presented the worst case analysis, which its critics argued was a caricature of the city's real financial position. The report allows one to judge that criticism of the Labour council. It also must be said that, although the discussions were much fuller in 1984, it was not the first time that Liverpool had made its arguments to Government. In fact, city officials had been making annual visitations to the Department of the Environment in Marsham Street ever since 1978 to present their case, both about the broad impact of public expenditure cuts on Liverpool's economic problems, and more specifically after 1981 about the adverse effect of the new grant system upon the city's finances.

Each time the Government thanked its visitors and reassured them in the words of Alfred Stocks, the chief executive, that it would 'bear it in mind next year.' But it never did until Labour gave it a more forceful reminder in 1984. By the time the Labour council offered its illegal challenge to the Government, senior officials could hardly argue that more conventional forms of persuasion would be more effective. Even though they were absolutely opposed to illegality, Liverpool's senior officers believed that Labour's argument had a lot of validity, and they were increasingly frustrated by their inability to persuade the Government. The knowledge of their officials' frustration encouraged the Labour group a little further along the road to confrontation.

The objections – Liverpool in the penalty area

Liverpool's officials had two basic objections to the grant system. One was the impact of the target and penalty system upon the city. The other was the way in which the Government assessed the city's need to spend when it calculated how much money it should be given. Liverpool's objection to the target system was that it discriminated against the city because it had originally been quite arbitrarily based on expenditure levels in one year, 1978/79. All authorities had been asked to cut back spending from that base year. But this ignored that fact that the city's spending that year was already low because it had behaved 'responsibly' during the 1970s and it had held down its spending. The target forced the city to cut its expenditure for a second time again in the 1980s. While Liverpool was being penalised by a cut in grant because of its earlier financial responsibility, other cities with similar needs were being treated much more generously by the target system. This unfairness was aggravated by the fact that Liverpool's targets and penalties were more severe because the city also spent beyond the Government's assessment of need figure. Liverpool's officials argued that this figure was too low in the first case. For the Government to use it to toughen the penalty was a double indemnity for the city. The targets were, in Reddington's words, 'arbitrary and punitive.'

The argument about Liverpool's target figure is closely connected to the city's politics during the 1970s and early 1980s. The target system was designed to control the high spending of Labour controlled cities, which the Government argued had been inefficient and profligate since the mid 1970s. But during this period, as we have seen, Liverpool was run not by the Labour party but by a Liberal-Conservative coalition whose primary purpose was to hold down the rates and spending, much to Labour's distaste at the time. Table 1 shows that Liverpool was a high-rating authority while under Labour control – for example in 1971/72 its rates were 19 per cent above the national average and they rose as much as 45 per cent above in 1973/74. By contrast, spending fell rapidly towards the end of that decade when the Liberals were in power

Table 1: Liverpool's Rates Compared with Averages for England and Wales

Year	Liverpool	Average	Difference
	p in £	p in £	%
1960/61	18.8	16.5	14
1965/66	23.8	21.3	12
1970/71	31.7	29.0	9
1971/72	39.7	33.2	19
1972/73	46.5	37.0	26
1973/74	58.5	40.3	45
1974/75*	64.6	52.0	24
1975/76*	69.1	67.9	2
1976/77*	71.1	72.7	−2
1977/78*	82.0	80.0	3
1978/79*	86.1	85.0	1

* Liberal budget.

and by 1976/77 Liverpool's rates were 2 per cent below the national average. In fact between 1975 and 1979 rate increases failed to keep pace even with the rate of inflation. Table 2 shows that in 1976/77 Liverpool's domestic rate increase was only 4 per cent compared with a 25.2 per cent increase in the retail price index. The city's rate increases were larger after 1979, but the greatest part of that increase is explained by the fact that by this time the city was compensating from its own resources for the cuts in central government support.

Also, the Liberals in their concern to hold down the rates made relatively small contingency provisions and often incurred budget deficits, as the income they raised failed to meet expenditure. This happened in six years out of ten between 1974 and 1983. Unlike many other high-rating Labour local authorities, during the 1970s Liverpool

Table 2: Domestic Rate Increases in Liverpool 1975–1983

Year	Rate increase	RPI increase
	%	%
1975/76	–	–
1976/77	4.0	25.2
1977/78	20.8	14.9
1978/79	6.4	13.1
1979/80	23.4	8.1
1975/1979	63.0	76.0
1979/80	–	–
1980/81*	50.6	17.3
1981/82	24.5	15.3
1982/83	16.0	12.6
1983/84	8.7	6.3
1979/1983	136.4	61.0

* Labour budget.

did not levy the kind of rates which produced large annual balances. As a result they did not build up the financial reserves which those other local authorities have been able to use during the early 1980s to help balance their budgets and avoid Government grant penalties. This again increased Labour's budget problems.

The impact upon the city's spending can be seen in table 3. Taking 1973/74 as a base year and controlling for inflation, it compares the growth in spending by Liverpool with that which the Government was willing to pay for, as well as with spending by other local authorities. Because of the Liberal's parsimony, Liverpool spent not merely less than other local authorities, but even less than Government guidelines indicated it should be spending. This became crucial to the argument about the city's finances, when the Government originally selected 1978/79 as a base for its expenditure target. To meet those Government targets, Liverpool has been obliged every year to cut back its expenditure from that already low level. If Liverpool's spending had gone up through the 1970s at the same rate as other local authorities or even according to Government guidelines, the city's target would have been much higher in 1984/85. And its difficulties in meeting the target and balancing the budget would have been far smaller.

However, the unfairness was worse than appeared. Despite the fact that its expenditure fell during the 1970s, in the first years of the grant system Liverpool cooperated with Government policy and made further

Table 3: Net Expenditure on Local Services

1973/74 = 100

	1974/75	1975/76	1976/77	1977/78	1978/79	1979/80
Liverpool district council	104.1	106.9	104.2	101.5	101.3	100.7
Government guidelines for:						
district authorities	101.8	109.3	112.8	115.3	115.9	118.9
all authorities	101.5	113.1	115.5	116.2	115.5	118.0
All local authorities	116.7	117.9	119.3	120.7	121.4	122.8

reductions. Other local authorities refused. They set out instead to break the new target system with a deliberate policy of high rather than low spending. The problems this caused eventually forced the Government to revise the system in 1982. This time it made local expenditure in 1981/82 the basis for future targets. This again penalised Liverpool, who had cooperated with the Government, because it was given another low target. By contrast, those authorities who had refused to cooperate, and had 'overspent' their original target, were set correspondingly higher targets.

As a result, in 1984/85 the total target figure in real terms for all English authorities was only 6 per cent lower than their expenditure in 1980/81. Liverpool's target was 11 per cent lower. Liverpool's officials calculated that between 1978/79 and 1983/84 the city had lost between £m26 and £m34 in Government grant as a direct result of penalties being imposed for spending over its target. This was the £m30 that the Labour council claimed the Government had 'stolen' from Liverpool and was demanding back. Officials argued that if the Government would take into account the city's financial behaviour throughout the whole rather than just half the decade, and adjust the target system to a 1974/75 base, Liverpool's financial problems would be solved immediately.

City officials argued that if the target system was fair, Liverpool would be treated no worse than any other city. But this was not the case. They illustrated this point by making a comparison with Manchester – a very similar city to Liverpool. In 1974/75, the first year of the new local councils, Manchester's expenditure was £m81 in comparison with Liverpool's £m79. Because of the Liberals' financial restraint in 1978/79 Liverpool was spending only £m125. Under a Labour council Manchester's spending had gone up to £m147. Since the cities' targets were originally tied to expenditure in that year, Liverpool had been given a target for 1984/85 of £m216, but Manchester's target was set at £m245. This was despite the fact that Manchester's assessment of need made by the Government was actually £m4 lower than Liverpool's. City officials argued that Liverpool's target should have moved in the same way as Manchester's to £m245 in 1984/85. That would reduce what the Labour council would need to raise from the rates by almost £m60. They also argued that if the comparison was made with not just one, but with all metropolitan district councils, based upon the average increases in expenditure since 1974/75, Liverpool should be given a target of £m243. Again, that target would wipe out its budget problems at a stroke.

For all these reasons, the Liverpool professionals believed that the Government's grant regime was asking the city to do more financially than was sensible. The target was already a very crude device to cut local spending. Its effect upon the city was even cruder. It was difficult for officials to persuade local Labour politicians to behave reasonably when the Government's own system seemed so unreasonable. They had a point. The anomalies of the target system reinforced the Labour politicians' worries and resentment of the city's economic decline. To them it made a bad situation worse and seemed politically provocative. It encouraged their belief in the moral correctness of their stand against the Government. In Tony Byrne's words, the target system was 'wicked and evil.'

Measuring social need in a declining city

The second part of the officials' case concerned what they called 'the flaws and inequities' of the grant system to which they had 'repeatedly drawn the Government's attention at length and in detail' and to 'the serious cumulative effect which this had had upon the finances of the council.' Their claim was that Liverpool had again suffered unfairly because since the grant system had been introduced in 1981/82, Liverpool's assessment of need had gone up by only 8.5 per cent. The average increase for all metropolitan districts had been 14 per cent, and for all local authorities it had been 17 per cent. In 1984/85 Liverpool's grant was £m198 as opposed to £m196 for 1983/84, a cash increase of less than 1 per cent and a reduction in real terms closer to 10 per cent. The average grant for all other local authorities in 1984/85 had declined by only 6 per cent in real terms. This loss of grant in Reddington's view meant the indicators used to determine need, and the importance it attached to them, were inadequate. It also meant that other measures of social need, which would benefit Liverpool more, were excluded.

The city's main objection to the way need was assessed was the assumption that, since the city's population had fallen dramatically, its need to spend, and therefore its grant from the Government, should fall more or less at the same rate. Liverpool's officials insisted that its need to spend money did not necessarily drop at the same rate as the population did. Partly this was because the remaining population was more socially needy and more expensive to provide for. Also historic service commitments for a larger population could not automatically be reduced as the population fell. A decline in population imposed costs which could not always be avoided in the short term. Grant calculations based on the size of the city's population at a single point in time seriously underestimated Liverpool's real need to spend.

The city argued that, for the same reason, the Government's use of Liverpool's relatively high expenditure per head of population in comparison with other local authorities as an indicator of its inefficiency, was equally unfair. Liverpool did spend more on some of its services. There were many reasons why this was so. Inefficiency might be only part of the reason. There was also the larger argument about the rate at which public sector organisations can adjust to change and cut back historic spending commitments. Liverpool's officers believed that the Government's estimates of how quickly local expenditure could be reduced when the city's population had been falling so rapidly, were wildly over-optimistic. Whoever was right in this technical argument, the result was that Liverpool got less grant than its officials felt was fair.

Liverpool's primary case was that, whatever safeguards were built in to the grant system, it broadly assumed that a drop in the city's population led to an increase in the resources available for those who remained and a drop in the authority's total costs. This is because the grant system, although very complex, rests on a very simple assumption. In order to get some indication of the prosperity or needs of an authority, the total rateable value of all properties in an authority is divided by its population to give a rateable value per head. In 1984 the Government declared a norm for this of £166.70. If an authority's actual figure is lower than this, it is considered 'poor', and if it is greater it is considered 'advantaged'. All the grant calculations are geared to bringing an authority's grant towards that standard figure. The advantaged areas receive less, and the poor areas receive more. That seems fair.

But there is a catch in this arrangement for declining cities like Liverpool. The rateable valuation of all properties was last carried out nationally in 1973. Since then the levels of economic activity and the general wealth in Liverpool have fallen dramatically. However, assessed rateable values have not, and remain at the 1973 levels. Using that measure, Liverpool seems richer than it is. Other cities which have prospered since 1973, seem poorer than they are for grant calculation purposes, because their rateable values have not been increased to take that new prosperity into account. That unfairness is aggravated by the fact that the Government 'norm' is calculated by dividing this outdated, inaccurate 1973 rateable value, by an up-to-date, accurate 1984 population figure. In Liverpool's case this is 60,000 smaller than in 1973. As a result, Liverpool appears to be far more 'advantaged' than it really is and receives less grant than is fair. In the same way, flourishing places with rising populations, but with artificially lower rateable values, get more grant than is fair. Since Liverpool has suffered the greatest economic decline and the highest loss of population of any big city in the country, the discrimination against it by the grant calculations is even worse than against other cities with similar but less severe problems.

Liverpool also argued that with a large and rapid drop in population the unit costs of providing local services did not decline; they went up. The city could not reduce revenue expenditure, or the historic costs of capital expenditure, at the same rapid rate as the population declined. In the short term, the same number of staff had to be paid, the same number of schools, libraries, old people's homes and public buildings had to be heated and maintained. The same miles of roads had to be swept. Often the same number of bins emptied – there were fewer people but often the same number of households. The same substantial interest charges had to be paid upon the city's long term capital debts, which had been originally used to build a city for a much larger population. Even in the long term, debts did not go away just because the people had.

As Michael Reddington often pointed out, the problems of financing a city whose population had dropped rapidly from a much higher level down to half a million were quite different from those of running a city with a relatively stable, or slowly growing, half a million population. In the longer term, the city could be expected to reduce staff and buildings. But things like school closures could be controversial, protracted and costly. Their practicality depended upon complicated issues – the age composition of the staff, the rate of population decline in different parts of the city, or school catchment areas, over which the authority had no control. There might be fewer children in every school. But that did not mean that one could close all classes for 9 year olds and make large savings.

The treasurer made this point with the example of education, by far the largest item of local expenditure. Between the financial years 1981/82 and 1982/83 the city's assessment of need was reduced by £m4.5, because the population in the city had fallen. Of that, £m3.25 was accounted for by education alone. In other words, the Government assumed that because it had to teach fewer children, Liverpool needed to spend less on education and could reduce its expenditure by £m3.25 in one year. However, the historic evidence contradicted this. Education costs had never contracted in that way in Liverpool.

For example, in 1958 the cost of educating a pupil in the Liverpool schools was 2 per cent below the national average. By 1982 it was 10 per cent above the average. However, the reasons were complicated. By 1982/83 the city's school population had fallen by 35 per cent – the overall national drop had been only 18 per cent. During this period the city had reduced its 'variable' costs, mainly staff salaries, more or less at the same rate as its population fell, by 31 per cent. It had only been able to reduce its 'fixed costs' – debt charges, maintenance costs, rents and rates – by about 12 per cent. The result was that in 1982/83, Liverpool's 'variable' costs were only 2.5 per cent above the national average. But the 'fixed' element was 32 per cent greater than the national average. In other words, despite making reductions where it could, in staffing, the difficulty of reducing 'fixed' costs had forced up the price of educating a child in Liverpool. The same difficulties would limit the rate of future reductions. In that light, the Government's grant cut of £m3.25 in 1982/83 was harsh.

Part of this problem was that the peculiarities of Liverpool's politics had prevented any administration getting a majority for any scheme to reorganise secondary education during the 1970s. This meant that in the 1980s the city provided too many school places and the service was far more expensive than it ought to be. As the Government rightly pointed out, that was Liverpool's own problem and it knew what it had to do to get its costs down. In fact, by 1985 the Labour administration had done this. However, the Government itself had actually contributed to the city's problem here. Since 1978, Liverpool had presented proposals to the Government for reorganising secondary schools on three separate occasions. Each time the Secretary of State had refused the city permission to implement them fully. Whatever the educational merits of those decisions, in this way the Government had contributed to Liverpool's failure to cut spending. Now it was penalising them for it.

Also the Government argued that since during the 1970s local authorities had levied high rates in order to build up cash reserves on which they now earned interest, it was legitimate to reduce the total grant by a comparable figure. The Government simply assumed without checking that all authorities had such balances and reduced all their grants accordingly. However, as we have seen, Liverpool had behaved in a conservative, financially responsible way in the past, and had not accumulated substantial balances. This meant in the first place that, unlike other authorities, it did not have these reserves to spend to cushion itself from the impact of grant cuts in the 1980s. But to add insult to injury, its grant was still actually reduced as if it did have them.

Local officials were not only worried by the inadequacies of existing measures of need. They were equally concerned about the city's particular needs that were not taken into account but which, if they were included, would bring Liverpool more grant money. For example, no allowance was made in the grant for the heavy costs incurred in running a major port health authority, in providing a regional library service or cleaning a major teaching hospital. Also when calculating the city's education grant, the Government did not count the number of places actually provided in nursery schools, special schools or further education. Instead, it simply inferred provision from the local population – the number of children under five, the school population or the adult population. Liverpool argued that greater social need in the city – the larger numbers of children at risk or higher rates of unemployment – meant it provided these services at a much higher rate than the national average. If the actual provision was counted, the authority would receive more grant for providing more places. The same applied in the field of mental illness and mental and physical handicap, where provision in inner city areas was liable to be higher than the national average, and actual measures of provision would bring the city more money.

More generally, officials argued that one of the crucial features of the city's decline was very high rates of unemployment, which imposed greatly increased demands upon its social services, adult and further education, and library and recreational services. The city simply had to provide more of these for a community without work. No specific allowance was made for this factor in the grant. Most important, the grant system made no particular allowance for those cities which because of their unique concentration of social, environmental and economic deprivation, the Government had identified as needing special treatment via the urban programme. In particular, the Government's recent emphasis in the urban programme on economic decline and regeneration made the absence of a sufficient unemployment or low-income factor in the block grant calculation even more unintelligible. Liverpool argued powerfully that if direct measures of economic deprivation were given the weight they deserved, the city would get much more grant money from the Government.

Overall, officials calculated that since the Conservatives had taken office in 1979, Liverpool had lost grant in four different ways. Liverpool had had to pay heavy penalties for spending over its target. It had also suffered because the way the grant was distributed between different kinds of local authorities had moved money away from the cities. On top of that, the Government had failed to increase its grant in line with the level of inflation. And it had also reduced the overall percentage of local spending it would fund. Local officials calculated the combined effect of all these upon the city was that it had lost £m116 in 1983 figures.

Of course, these technical disputes constantly exercise all those involved in giving and getting grants. They are part of the common currency of that debate. There is no single formula which could meet the diverse interests within and between central and local government. But many of the city's arguments were good ones. They also argued that while such disagreements of definition were inevitable and perhaps legitimate when an authority's grant was being decided, it was quite a different matter when the results were also used to determine its expenditure targets. The Government has always characterised Liverpool as an overspender in relation to its assessed need. Its targets and penalties have been harsher as a result. These differences in definition became much more important politically when they contributed to the city's financial problems and the larger political conflict about them. The city's case was persuasive on two counts. The assumptions of the grant system were unsympathetic to the problems of both population loss and of economic decline. The Government's policy failed to help the city as much as might be expected in these two respects – they are two key dimensions of urban decline. For Liverpool's politicians, they were also two of the most visible indicators of the city's decline. Like their objections to the target system, this fact only reinforced Labour politicians' refusal to collaborate in a policy which seemed to worsen an already difficult situation.

The civil servants' reply

Civil servants were wholly unsympathetic to Liverpool officials' arguments. They were particularly sceptical of the claim that it had 'lost' £m116 in grant since 1979/80. This was based, in their view, on the quite unjustifiable assumption that the Government's financial support for the city should be fixed for all time at the 1979/80 level, whereas everyone knew that Government policy had changed since then, and the reductions in grant support had been made 'as a deliberate act to strengthen local accountability.' Liverpool was not treated differently from any other authority when its assessment of need was calculated. In fact its per capita need assessment was the fourth highest of any metropolitan district.

Nor would the civil servants accept that the fall in the city's share of the national grant total was evidence of inequity in the system. It was Government policy to reduce local government spending and central government's contribution to it.The size of the national cake had fallen and Liverpool's slice with it. An individual authority's share of grant could fall for a variety of reasons – because of changes in its resources, changes in its expenditure level or in its level of need. It was true that Liverpool's assessment and grant had fallen. This was not the result of any discrimination – merely the application of the general rules for allocating Government grant. Since 1981/82 Liverpool's need assessment had fallen by 1 per cent. This had been caused by several things: there had been an above average reduction in the number of secondary school pupils; the 1981 Census had provided more accurate information about its smaller population; the doubling of the weight given to the ethnic minority population in measuring additional needs had benefited other authorities more than Liverpool; and housing need had fallen because of a drop in interest rates and increases in rents which had reduced the subsidy paid from general rates.

Despite this fall, civil servants pointed out that Liverpool's assessment was still 10 per cent higher than the average of all metropolitan districts and only three cities in the country had a higher one. They argued that the question of measures of need was always under review by the grant working group of central and local government officials, and the city could take its arguments there if it wanted to change the rules. However, as they also admitted, the politics of grant allocation were fierce, because 'any improvements in the city's position would be balanced by losses to other authorities.' In other words, with the total grant limited and declining, the Government could always play off one set of local interests against another, which would make Liverpool's case difficult to win.

Civil servants argued essentially that the arrangements were fixed and Liverpool would have to live within the rules as everyone else did. The city's officials' argument was that the rules were discriminatory, even if they had to be accepted. Liverpool's politicians' view was that the rules were there to be broken if they were discriminatory. At least two of the Government's defences of Liverpool's grant were worth an argument. It was quite clearly ignoring the city's major claim that its expenditure did not decline as rapidly as its population fell. In particular, the city's inability to cut the costs of education in response to falling school rolls was obviously being particularly heavily penalised by grant reduction in the 1980s, despite the good case it had made about educational expenditure.

The Government also admitted that the way in which ethnic minorities are counted for grant purposes penalised Liverpool. The city has a substantial black population, estimated between 20,000 and 40,000, which suffers well documented, racial disadvantage. Since the majority are not recent immigrants, but long-standing residents, they are not counted in Government measures of ethnic deprivation. Liverpool had argued for a long time that this anomaly prevented the city taking advantage of the most important source of Government money for dealing with racial disadvantage, Section II of the 1966 Local Government Act, as well as giving it less block grant than it should have. It seemed unreasonable at best that only one year after the Toxteth riots, this was further aggravated by changes in the grant which gave other cities more money for ethnic minorities.

The Department's reply to the city's argument about targets and penalties was even less sympathetic. It merely restated the obvious point that the general rules had been applied to the city as to everywhere else and that Liverpool had lost £m14 in the two years 1982–84. The Government imposed lower targets on those authorities who had spent above their assessment of need, and their targets in previous years, compared with those who had not. Liverpool knew this but had still spent above both its assessment and target figures and had therefore been penalised. The responsibility, they argued, was 'entirely in the hands of the local authority.' This reply simply ignored the two key elements in the city's claim. The first was that the targets were discriminatory because of the choice of low base years which inevitably had made it difficult for Liverpool to make the necessary reductions and avoid penalties in successive years. The second was that the calculations of need were insensitive to Liverpool's problems and, while they might be used simply to allocate money, they should not be used in determining targets and therefore penalties.

Equally, officials simply rejected Liverpool's comparison of its target with Manchester's. They just would not accept that 'a single comparison with a particular authority over a particular period of time provides a valid basis for arguing that Liverpool's target is unfair or unreasonable.' But they offered no justification for their view, even though it could be argued that the similarities between the two cities made the comparison a sensible, if not a precise, test of the fairness or reasonableness of the target system. Also, the city had made comparisons of its targets with not one, but all metropolitan districts, which had strengthened its case. The Government again simply ignored this.

In defence of Liverpool's 1984/85 target, civil servants argued that 35 authorities had received larger cuts than Liverpool in their targets that year compared with the previous year's figure. This was disingenuous. The Government knew that Liverpool's 1983/84 target had been much lower than its actual expenditure. The Liberal administration that year had agreed to meet the target, without specifying how the necessary large reductions in expenditure would be made. The target had not been met in 1983/84. Labour had spent above it, incurred penalties and run up a deficit which made it even more difficult to stay within the new target. In other words, it was the cumulative impact of target reductions, not those in a single year which was important. The civil servants must have appreciated that.

Liverpool's claims about the target system were well founded, even though the civil servants could not afford to admit it. The best they could argue was that the system had to begin at some year, and the Government had chosen the year it had taken office. There were bound to be anomalies. This was not a very persuasive case. The fact that the Government abandoned the whole target system in 1985 only strengthened the Liverpool professionals' claims about the arbitrariness of the system. While it does not necessarily justify the Labour council's behaviour, it does explain why they were so reluctant to play the game when they thought the rules were so unfair. Labour may have been looking for an argument, but the target system provided them with a perfect excuse.

Balancing the books – Liverpool's requests

Apart from rehearsing the opposing views of the origins of Liverpool's problems, the discussions also looked at proposals for resolving the immediate financial crisis. They became the basis for a settlement in 1984. The city was mainly looking for extra money. The Government was mainly looking for economies through increased efficiency and creative accountancy. Unlike their politicians, Liverpool's officials accepted that their grant and target had been set by Parliament for 1984/85 and could not be changed for that year. They were hoping for some changes on those issues in the 1985/86 settlement. For 1984/85 they were trying to get Government help from outside the main grant system in four areas: exemptions from grant penalties for certain kinds of city spending, extra aid from the urban programme, increased money for housing and relief from housing debt charges.

The city's first request concerned the special power the Minister had to exclude or 'disregard' any local authority's spending over target when he calculated its grant penalties. In 1984/85 Patrick Jenkin was planning to 'disregard' only four kinds of spending by local authorities: increases in urban programme expenditure, expenditure on schemes jointly financed with health authorities, expenditure on civil defence and the costs to local authorities of policing the miners' strike. City officials wanted the Minister to extend this exclusion to a range of Liverpool's spending. They argued that the Government's target figure for the city in 1984/85 was based on Liverpool's planned budget expenditure in

1981/82. However, in keeping with Liberal administration's strategy at the time, those figures had both underestimated the real costs of paying for the city's services and exaggerated its likely income. As a result, expenditure that year, as in succeeding years, had been far greater than the planned figure. Liverpool's officials argued that the city's actual, not its intended, expenditure was a more reasonable base for the Government to set the city's target and its grant penalties.

The difference between the planned and final expenditure in the three years since 1981/82 added up to £m35 above the target figures. This had lost the city £m54 in grant because of the penalties imposed for overspending. Officials argued that this loss reflected the insensitivity of the national target system to Liverpool's particular local problems. They asked the Minister to 'disregard' retrospectively that £m35, as well as £m18 for 1984/5. Once penalties were taken into account, this would reduce the burden on the city's rates that year by £m38. The civil servants argued such exemptions could not be given to Liverpool alone but would have to apply to all local authorities. The disregards the Minister had decided to make nationally only added up to £m17 in total, whereas the cost of Liverpool's proposals would be over £m100. The suggestions were rejected on cost grounds. Although civil servants might also have argued this was a particular form of special pleading from Liverpool to compensate for the Liberals' financial inadequacies over the years.

City officials also wanted more money for housing, arguing that the Government's restrictions on its housing investment programme in recent years had dramatically reduced Liverpool's ability to build new houses. Because of the extra pressure upon its limited housing resources, the Labour council had decided that in future it would not use its housing programme to pay for repairs to existing property, because this directly reduced the amount of money it had to build new houses. Instead of 'capitalising' £m5.6 worth of repairs in 1983/84 in this way and borrowing the money long term, as the previous Liberal budget had planned, the Labour party was planning to pay for it, as well as a further £m8 in 1984/85, from its revenue budget. This would give the city an extra £m13.6 for building new houses in 1984/85.

Equally it would add the same amount to its revenue budget that year. That would cause a huge deficit, if Labour refused to increase the rates to pay for this new expenditure. City officials wanted the Government to increase its housing allowance for the two years by £m13.6 to avoid that deficit. Again the civil servants refused to help. They argued that there was nothing left from other councils' underspending in 1983/84. And everything for 1984/85 had already been allocated. Instead they argued that the council should speed up its sale of council houses so that it could use the proceeds to finance new house building. This proved especially ironic later in the year when the argument about housing resources was reopened and the Government cut what the city could spend that way. The report pointed out that the Minister planned to visit the city at some point to examine its housing problems and resource needs for 1985/86. Although it was not known at the time, this would help change the course of the confrontation. The promise of money for housing became a central element in the budget saga the whole of next year. Although the Government refused these first two major request for aid for 1984/85, Liverpool's two other requests for urban programme money and relief from some housing debt interest charges received a rather more favourable response, and were crucial to the final settlement, as we shall see.

Government's search for economies

The joint talks also gave Government officials a chance to go through the city's books in great detail and to suggest a number of ways in which Labour's planned 1984/5 deficit budget could be reduced. They recommended that Labour should abandon all its new spending proposals. This would immediately cut the total by £m10.25. The city could also make technical changes in the way it repaid debt charges by switching from equal annual instalments to a sinking fund method, which could save between £m0.8 and £m3.6. Most important, the city could save £m13.6 from its revenue budget by 'capitalising' housing repairs in 1983/84 and 1984/85, as the Liberal administration had planned. Civil servants also argued that, although the city planned to use £m7.2 from its reserves, they had found a further £m7.3 in various special funds whcih the city could use in 1984/85. These changes would reduce the size of the budget problem enormously. But even if all those measures were taken to cut expenditure and reduce grant loss, the civil servants had to admit that Liverpool would still need a rate increase of between 59 per cent and 84 per cent.

Government officials also suggested Liverpool should raise its rents in keeping with Government guidelines. Labour was refusing to do this because the city's rents were higher than any city outside London as a result of previous Liberal policies. But the city lost grant because of this decision not to increase. Officials also told the city to sell off corporate assets, which would reduce its debt charges, even though it would lead to a future loss of rent. Liverpool should freeze employment and should not fill staff vacancies, a Liberal practice which Labour had abandoned. It should implement an early retirement policy and introduce a voluntary redundancy policy, even though there would be initial costs because of redundancy payments. Civil servants calculated these measures could save the authority between £m4–7 a year. If that budget figure was reached, the increase in the city's rate could be held to between 37 per cent and 71 per cent.

As well as their reactions to the city's immediate crisis, the 'joint report' also revealed the civil servants general view of Liverpool as the worst kind of local authority – inefficient, overstaffed and expensive. Even a stripped down budget would still be 16–20 per cent higher than their assessment of what the city needed to spend. And as they were at constant pains to point out, Liverpool's costs for education, personal social services, recreation, environmental health and refuse collection were higher than average metropolitan district costs, because of the city's 'inefficiency.' In their view, the budget problem was partly the result of a political gesture but partly a result of long-term managerial weaknesses which made the city's services far more expensive than they should be. Civil servants suggested a number of areas for immediate economies: reorganising the refuse collection, rationalising the education service in keeping with its plans for secondary school reorganisation and reducing the size of the direct labour organisation.

City officials were not happy with the civil servants' suggestions. One of their primary objections was that Government comparisons of local authority expenditure on a per capita basis were quite misleading because they ignored the effects of a declining population. Since fixed costs could not always be reduced quickly, the Government could not argue that high spending proved that Liverpool was simply 'inefficient' in that blanket fashion. As the city officials pointed out, and as the civil servants had to accept, the Government's proposals all had longer-term costs for the city. Changing the method of repaying debt charges would lead to higher interest charges in the future. 'Capitalising' housing repairs meant that fewer resources would be available to finance the house building programme. It also meant that in seven years the extra interest charges could add up to the original cost of repairs, and would then incur even greater Government penalties for higher city spending. The final costs to the ratepayer in real terms would be very much greater. Finally, if all its financial reserves were used in one year 1984/85, it would obviously mean they would not be available in future years. The treasurer estimated that if the city used them in 1984/85, it could need a 45 per cent rate increase in 1985/86 just to make up for them. In other words, the Government proposals might ease the city's difficulties in 1984/85. But only at the expense of storing up financial problems for the future.

Which side won?

The review dramatically revealed the two sides' radically different perceptions of the city's financial problems. City officials were concerned with the harsh effects of the Government grant system which was insensitive to the city's problems. The civil servants focused on the internal managerial failings of the authority and the range of options that were open to the Labour council, but which it had rejected on political grounds. To some extent, these differences stemmed from different time horizons – city officials were anxious to stress long-term impacts, civil servants to emphasise short-term solutions. Publicly and privately, both believed they had won the argument.

The Government might have won the argument about whether Liverpool faced an unavoidable budget crisis, which could not be resolved without draconian policies or consequences in 1984. There were things the city could do. But Liverpool surely won the larger argument that it was facing major financial problems which were aggravating its even larger economic and social problems and that Government policies, especially the target system, were making that bad situation worse. The city's financial options were gradually being eliminated year by year. And from Labour's point of view, there was a clear political rationale for dramatising the position and resisting the Government from the outset, rather than collaborating in the sacrifices year after year. And as we have seen, public opinion in Liverpool certainly saw the issue in those terms.

The 'joint report' in many ways confirmed this. Even when rejecting the city's larger complaints about the grant system, and recommending measures which they knew would impose longer-term costs, the civil servants could not produce a balanced budget for 1984/85 which did not mean further sacrifices for the city or substantial rate rises. The newspaper headline 'Whitehall Whiz Kids stumped' was quite accurate. The 'joint report' showed both sides had good points to make. But Liverpool had more of them than the Government. There are no easy solutions for dealing with the problems of a city in rapid decline like Liverpool. However, this review suggested that the Government's grant system was worsening, not helping, them. And it encouraged the Labour council in its resistance, which now believed it had technical as well as moral right on its side. As Tony Byrne claimed 'it has been proved time and time again this year that our interpretation of the facts and figures has been correct. Any analysis will prove us to be absolutely right.'

The discussions also had an important political effect. The Labour leadership trapped the Government into becoming much more deeply embroiled in the city's problems and politics than it wished to be, or was good for it. As long as the Government could remain aloof from the local implications of its grant system the contradictions within it remained hidden. But once it became directly involved in the details of Liverpool's financial affairs, the Government was bound to get into trouble. It could not deny the problems were real, and it could find no easy solutions to them. The distance which typically separates central and local government has genuine political benefits for the centre. And these were lost by the Government. Even Labour's opponents could see how they had revealed the vulnerability of the Government on these issues.

Despite all these issues, the negotiations became the basis of Liverpool's 1984 budget settlement. The city's requests for extra money, and the civil servants' suggestions for cuts in the deficit budget and long-term economies, all formed part of the deal. After the 'joint report' was produced in early June, a package was drawn up by the Ministers who had been monitoring the negotiations. They were formalised in a letter in late June from Patrick Jenkin to John Hamilton and allowed the Labour council to make a quite different legal budget in early July. If it had been hard for the Government to get Liverpool to agree to compromise, the presentation of the final deal proved even more difficult. It soured political relations between the two sides from then on. In particular, it focused the Labour council, especially its Militant deputy leader, Derek Hatton, in Margaret Thatcher's sights. From that point they were never far off her long term agenda.

CONCESSIONS AND CONTROVERSY – The July 1984 Settlement

5

The months of tension and negotiations were finally ended in July 1984 when the Labour group at last made a budget and set a rate, four months into the financial year. Instead of the threatened 170 per cent, the rate rise was 17 per cent. Despite all the talk of legal action by the district auditor, the courts or the Attorney General, and of municipal bankruptcy, nothing had happened to Liverpool. No one had moved against them. The financial institutions continued to lend. The Public Works Loan Board continued to lend. The Government paid the rate support grant. Council tenants paid their rent. Many ratepayers paid their rates even though none had been levied. The budget was finally set amidst a welter of claims and counter-claims which seemed designed to confuse the outside world, as both sides claimed a political and financial victory.

The deal on which Liverpool's legal budget was based was spelt out in a confidential letter from Patrick Jenkin to John Hamilton written on 29 June. The two sides met in London on 9 July to agree the details and finalise the agreement. At the end of the meeting, the Government's understanding was that the details would be kept secret until the Labour group presented its revised legal budget to the council on 11 July. It would then be quite clear what both sides had had to give up to get a legal budget. But in the Government's eyes Liverpool reneged on that arrangement both by the timing of its announcement and the way it presented the deal publicly, as it set out to extract the maximum political capital from it.

Immediately after the meeting on 9 July, the Liverpool delegation returned home to present the package in the evening to the district Labour party for its endorsement. Having got that, the leaders emerged from the meeting with clenched fists raised to face the television cameras and the crowds chanting the miners' hymn 'Here we go'. And they began to publicise the Government's offer in the most favourable light to themselves. Even at the time, many in the party doubted the wisdom of the leaders' crowing over the Government in this way. But they pressed on. It led one civil servant at the time to exclaim 'I'd like to see the lot of them locked up in gaol.'

The claims and counter claims

Party leader John Hamilton argued that the Government's concessions would be worth £m50 to Liverpool. Finance chairman Tony Byrne, put it even higher, arguing that the immediate concessions, combined with budget adjustments which would be made in view of Government promises of future aid, could make the deal worth £m60 to £m90. Replying to Patrick Jenkin's protestations that no specific promises had been made about future years, he said 'What do you expect a very battered Tory minister to be saying?' But that issue was to return with a vengeance later in the year. The powerful Militant leader of the district Labour party, Tony Mulhearn, called it 'a major U-turn by this Government' which emphasised the lessons for Labour's national leadership who had sat on the fence during the crisis. Most provocatively, Derek Hatton argued that Margaret Thatcher and Patrick Jenkin had 'bottled out' of a confrontation with Liverpool, and it was only a matter of time before Jenkin resigned or Thatcher sacked him. 'There is no way' he claimed, 'even Thatcher can take on the might of the working class in this city. And this is just the start. Next year we will see not only the defeat of rate-capping and the plans to cut the metropolitan councils, but we will start to see the kicking out of Thatcher herself.' That bold claim permanently altered the way the Conservatives would view and treat Liverpool in future.

Other Labour councils did not miss the point either. Sheffield's leader, David Blunkett, promptly emphasised its relevance to the Government's rate-capping plans, arguing 'it could mean up to a dozen Liverpools next year and it is Ministers who will have to pay the price.' The Labour councillors, he argued, had 'shamed' Mr Jenkin into a substantial climbdown. Ted Knight, leader of Lambeth, added 'I think Jenkin is just floundering. The concessions he has made to Liverpool will strengthen the fight of other Labour authorities in the coming year.' Even the Liberals weighed in as David Alton, the sole Liverpool Liberal MP, argued that the Government had sent the message out to moderates that it 'will give in to intimidation, blackmail, bludgeoning, and the threat of riots.'

Mrs. Thatcher was infuriated by Labour's behaviour. In her view they had broken the agreement and grossly exaggerated the settlement. She was not to forgive them for the trouble it caused her, as she had to defend the deal in Parliament to friends and foes alike. One Conservative backbencher put the feeling most clearly 'More public attention has been devoted to that area in recent years than to anywhere else and the only result has been ever more whining and whinging from the left wing commissars there, and the rest of the country's ratepayers and taxpayers are fed up with it.' Patrick Jenkin also did his best to defend the limited nature of the deal, angrily attacking Hatton and Labour for trying to 'dance on his political grave' and con the public into believing they had won a great victory. 'In fact,' he argued, 'they have had to eat their words. Their policy of confrontation and blackmail has failed.'

Others were also trying to play down the deal. Sir Trevor Jones, Liverpool's Liberal leader, with a different eye on the local repercussions, insisted Jenkin had made no real concessions. 'There is no new money,' he argued. 'They are merely trying to continue the confidence trick, but in fact it has been a massive climbdown by the Labour party.' The national Labour leadership, for different reasons, was equally anxious to minimise the deal, as well as to emphasise their own contribution to the negotiated settlement. They stressed the negotiations had only flourished once they had intervened. They still praised the defections of the 'sensible six' rebel councillors 'without whose action there would never even have been the opportunity to have the negotiations.' And reacting to the city's claim of total victory, John Cunningham warned, 'It would be barmy to exaggerate what the Government has given because the people will be able to see what the figures are.' The national leadership was as unhappy with Liverpool's presentation of the settlement as it had been with its behaviour throughout the crisis.

The two sides could hardly be further apart in their public claims. Whatever the facts and despite its protestations, the Government could only feel it had lost the propaganda battle. It had been trapped by the logic of its own grant system. To bend that system, it was bound to be seen as giving away either too much, or too little, too late. Everyone agreed the most important implication was for the coming year. It would encourage other Labour authorities and return to haunt the leadership of both national parties. In fact the process was already under way. The Labour Party's conference on local government was held in Sheffield the weekend before the Liverpool settlement was announced. The delegates had an early opportunity to see the confidential details with their apparent testimony to the results of municipal pressure. And it galvanised them. The reception given to Liverpool was much more favourable than it had been at a similar conference six months earlier in Nottingham, when the majority of speakers had been sceptical of Liverpool's case and its tactics. The conference, supported by Eric Heffer and John Cunningham, finally agreed a strategy of non-compliance with the Government's rate-capping in 1985.

The final resolution argued that Labour authorities had 'a legal obligation to provide services for the homeless, for elderly people and for children. They have a legal obligation to protect the public. If they comply with the Government they will be forced to break these obligations. In this context, non-compliance with the rates act is the only option to fulfil public responsibilities.' In this hardening of Labour's position, Liverpool had played an important part. Arguably, Liverpool's 'victory' in 1984 misled the other Labour authorities in their campaign against the Government in 1985. The overselling of Liverpool's success led the rest to overplay their hand and finally undermined them in 1985. Liverpool had been after a political and a financial victory in 1984. If it got the first, the second was more problematic.

Doing the deal: deficit budgets and legal budgets

Although other Labour authorities were encouraged by Liverpool's 'victory', who was telling the truth? Was there really enough in the deal to persuade other Labour councils to resist the Government in 1985 in a search for similar concessions? The scale of Labour's 'victory' and the Government's concessions can only be assessed by comparing Labour's original April 'deficit' budget with the legal one presented in July, along with the issues raised in the 'joint report' and Patrick Jenkin's letter to John Hamilton. The most important question is: how did the Labour council transform an apparently impossible financial position in April to an apparently manageable one in July? Had the Government bought them out of the dilemma? Indeed were the problems in any sense resolved, or merely defined away in July? If so, what implications did this have for the next financial year?

Labour's original 'deficit' budget for 1984/85 had been £m296.7. But how did Labour reach that figure when it was actually running the city in 1983/84 on the £m212 budget it had inherited from the Liberal party? Labour claimed that a large part of its problem stemmed from their predecessors' policies. In particular, it argued that the last Liberal budget which Labour had inherited had been financially unsound, because it underestimated the real costs of the city's services and its probable levels of expenditure. It would inevitably mean there would be a budget deficit at the end of the year, causing problems for 1984/85. In fact, when the Liberals were originally planning the budget for 1983/84 they arrived at a figure of £m234 which would have needed a rate rise of about 40 per cent. Eventually they settled on £m218. But the Government then set the city a target of £m212. To avoid large grant penalties, the Liberals reduced their planned expenditure to that figure.

But they did this, not by reducing the services but primarily by creative accountancy. They planned to use the authority's £m7 reserves which had been built up over the years, rather than increasing the rates. They also simply reduced planned expenditure for 1983/84 by £m6 without specifying where those 'unallocated cuts' would be made. They did not add to the cost of the 1983/83 budget the £m3 deficit that was actually being carried forward from 1982/83. Labour argued that this £m16 should have been included in the real cost of running the city in 1983/84 and the Liberal rate increase should have been much higher. In their view, and in that of the local authority unions, the Liberals' was an illegal 'deficit' budget from the time it was made. Whether that was true, the Labour council inherited a very messy and difficult financial position from the Liberal administration. The financial juggling act which the Liberals and Conservatives carried out during the 1970s and early 1980s finally caught up with the city. The self-interested search for votes in that lost decade sowed a bitter harvest for the 1980s.

But Labour did not try to implement the Liberal budget which it regarded as dishonest. Quite apart from this, the party claimed it had been elected in 1983 with a mandate to protect jobs and services, not to cut them. In the event, most of the Liberals' 'unspecified' savings of £m6 were never made by Labour. In its first year of office, it spent £m4.2

more than the Liberals had planned. Given their failures over the years to achieve the rate of savings they promised, there must be considerable doubt whether the Liberals could have achieved the £m6 savings in one year, even if they had run the city and had been actively trying to make economies. It was too optimistic and bound to run into problems. In 1983/84 Labour spent not £m212 but £m216. This became the base for the controversial 'deficit' budget which was primarily made by the party's finance spokesman Tony Byrne.

Labour's 'deficit' budget for 1984/85 was constructed by adding new items onto the previous year's. As table 1 shows, the original Liberal budget for 1983/84 had been £m212.3. Labour added to that £m11.1 to cover for inflation during that year. It then added the £m4.2 deficit which it had spent beyond the Liberals' figure .The real cost of existing services in 1984/85 prices was calculated by Labour as £m227.6, an expenditure of £m11 over target. It would cost that much just to stand still in 1984/85. And Labour planned to add an extra £m22 to that for new programmes.

But a third of that extra was actually intended to get into the base budget enough money to cover real commitments the city actually had, but for which no allowance had ever been made in Liberal budgets. For example, since Labour had not made the Liberals' unallocated cuts in 1983/84, it calculated that just over £m4 would have to be added to the 1984/85 budget to pay for existing services.

Also the Liberals throughout the 1970s, in their anxiety to minimise spending, had always assumed that local authority jobs would be lost by natural wastage and the freezing of vacancies. In fact, the assumed rate of loss had never been achieved and the city always had more employees on the payroll than the Liberal budget figures ever admitted existed. For 1984/85 Labour estimated that there were 350 'extra' employees on the staff and that their salaries would cost in the region of £m3. Labour intended to recognise the staff existed and incorporate that figure in the new budget. In other words, this £m7 was not for new policy commitments by Labour, but their calculation of the price of getting the city's budget on a sound financial footing after a decade of the failings of their Liberal predecessors.

But there were many new policies which the Labour party had chosen to put in the budget which swelled it enormously. In 1983 it had promised to create 1,000 new council jobs in its first year of office.

Labour had not, in fact, added that many to its regular payroll. But it had sponsored almost that number of people on Manpower Services Commission projects, and Labour promised that, as these lapsed after twelve months, it would employ the people on a permanent basis. That would cost £m3.4 in 1984/85. The policy was the Labour council's

Table 1: Labour's Deficit Budget for 1984/85 £m

Expenditure	
	£m
Total	296.7
Base budget	269.1
Real cost of 1983/84 budget	227.6
of which: original agreed	212.3
inflation	11.1
overspend	4.2
New growth	22.1
Housing repairs	8.6
Loss of grant	2.8
Inflation	8.0
Deficit	34.7
Less use of reserves	−7.1
Income	
Total	296.7
Grant	27.6
Rate required	269.1
9% rate levy	108.2
Shortfall*	160.9

* Equivalent to a rate increase of 170 per cent or 5,000 local authority employees' salaries.

response to the Liberals' shedding of council jobs in the 1970s and 1980s. But the costs to it were great.

An even larger, controversial item in Labour's budget was the 'decoration allowances' which they were planning to make to council house tenants. As we have seen, Labour constantly attacked the Liberals and Conservatives throughout the lost decade for starving public sector housing, and allowing the council rents to become the highest in the country outside London. In the 1983 election Labour had promised to cut rents by £2 a week and it devised a way to pay back council tenants some of their rent, which avoided the Government simply clawing it back through cuts in social security benefit to tenants. It had paid each tenant £16 as a 'decoration allowance' in compensation for their high rents. This had cost £m1 in 1983/84. The Labour council planned to do this again on a much larger scale in 1984/85 at a cost of £m8.5.

Patrick Jenkin used this as evidence that the council's financial problems were self-imposed. But it must also be seen in the political context in which for a decade the Liberals and Conservatives had consistently raised council house rents higher than central governments at the time thought necessary. In other words, they had subsidised the services and the rate payers at the expense of the rent payers. The Labour council was intending to redress the balance. But in the 1980s the price to the council in grant penalty for the extra £m8.5 involved was again very high.

Labour's finance chief, Tony Byrne, also planned to add £m8.6 to the budget because he refused to pay for housing repairs from the city's capital programme, charging it instead to the rates. This would create tremendous problems in balancing the budget once Government penalties of almost £m16 were added. But once again it has to be seen in the context of the Liberal and Conservative policies of the 1970s of abandoning the council house building programme. To compensate for that period, Labour wanted to expand its house building programmes dramatically. But if it used the capital programme, rather than the rates, to pay for housing repairs, this would seriously restrict the size of its building programme. On top of that, £m2.8 was added to cover the expected loss of Government money for urban programme projects which had had three years Government support, and were ineligible for any more. Liverpool planned to keep those projects going and pay for them from the rates. Finally £m8 was put into the budget to cover for inflation in the year 1984/85. Once these were added to the revised base budget, Labour planned to spend £m269.1 in 1984/85.

That figure was then reduced because Labour planned to spend in 1984/85 the £m7 from its reserves that the Liberals had originally intended to use in 1983–84. The reason was simple. The penalty system became progressively tougher each year, so that greater grant savings could be made by using the reserves in 1984/85 rather than in 1983/84. This would reduce penalty in 1984/85, but it would retrospectively increase expenditure and penalty in 1983/84. The deficit being carried forward into 1984/85, therefore, would be much higher than the Liberals had intended.

This reduced Labour's planned expenditure for 1984/85 to £m262. However, to that there had to be added the deficit from 1983/84 which Labour now calculated would be £m34, half of which was accounted for by penalties for overspending. Labour would have to cover the inherited £m34 deficit from the rates in 1984/85. Once added to the £m262 base budget, expenditure would reach £m296.7, with a huge loss of grant and the need for swingeing rate rises. That was the bargaining figure that Liverpool used with the Government through the spring of 1984. It was partly a product of unavoidable inherited difficulties and partly a result of its deliberate policy choices – all presented in the bleakest terms. This was what Labour reconstructed in order to get a settlement in July 1984, in response to the extra aid from Patrick Jenkin.

The Government's offer

But how much did the Government give Liverpool? The two sides had a bitter row about this, as we have seen. In fact, the Government gave four pieces of aid and a promise of future help in the crucial area of housing. The aid was offered in Patrick Jenkin's letter written to John Hamilton on June 29 after the professionals' negotiations. Jenkin's letter made it quite clear that the Government was not going to make any major concessions to Liverpool in the grant, target or penalty system, or its housing allocation for 1984/85. These had all been fixed and approved by Parliament. The Government was not giving way to pressure on those. But Jenkin did admit that he had some 'marginal flexibility' in the special urban programme money which he would use to help Liverpool over its short-term problems. First, the Government offered to allow up to £m3.1 of the city's urban programme money to be used to continue support for projects which otherwise Liverpool would have to support on the rates. Once reduced penalties for spending less over target had been taken into account, this would reduce the city's expenditure by £m7.5. Secondly, and 'in addition,' as Tony Byrne forever insisted, the Government added an extra £m2.5 to Liverpool's urban programme allowance of £m24. Again Jenkin admitted, once the penalties were included, this would reduce Liverpool's expenditure by a further £m7.

The third piece of Government help was in housing finance. Along with many other urban authorities, Liverpool had a large stock of high-rise buildings built in the 1950s and 1960s which had become so unpopular with tenants that the only solution, in many cases, was to demolish them. But if this was done, the city continued to pay interest charges on the money they had borrowed to build them, long after the flats were knocked down and the Government subsidy ended. The city asked the Government to ease this burden by giving it housing subsidy to cover those continuing interest charges, and to help with the actual costs of demolition.

Patrick Jenkin said he had already been considering this idea. He decided that he would change this in future, but it would apply to all authorities. No precise figure was put on this, but Liverpool calculated it would be worth about £m1.7 to them, or £m5 once penalties were taken into account. Finally, the Government would pay the city about £m1 for environmental works which had already been carried out in housing action areas and general improvement areas. In total, the aid given by the Government amounted to £m8.6. This would reduce its grant penalties by £m12. The package was actually worth just over £m20 to the city's revenue budget.

Although the amount was helpful, it was nowhere near the figure Liverpool had been after. The Government tried to suggest that it could all have been achieved through the normal processes of consultation, without the bankruptcy campaign. This seems doubtful. The aid for environmental improvements certainly was a mere accounting device and the talks only identified the amount and brought forward payment. The money would have been paid anyway. That was less clear in the case of the other three pieces of aid. It was true that local authorities had been pressing for a review of housing subsidy for demolished properties. However, they press governments for many things, without necessarily getting them. Liverpool's pressure at least encouraged or hastened the process of change.

The £m2.5 of urban programme money the Government gave Liverpool was obviously new. The status of the £m3.1 funding for the 'time expired' projects was less certain. It was true, as civil servants claimed, that the Government knew that 'time expiry' was a general problem in the urban programme and that any local authority could discuss it with them. But the experience of Liverpool and other authorities in the past, did not suggest that the Government was willing to help automatically with the 'time expiry' problem in this way. Indeed when some months later a number of inner London authorities argued that they would qualify for a large extra amount of grant if, like Liverpool they were given special support for their 'time expired' projects, the Government dismissed the claim. This money did help Liverpool. However, it did not mean that the city's urban programme allocation was increased by £m3.1. Liverpool was given greater discretion in the use of its existing money, but it was at the cost of new projects which might otherwise have been funded in 1984/85.

Labour's concessions

How was the deal worth the £m50 claimed by John Hamilton or the £m60–90 by Tony Byrne? The answer was that if the Government made some concessions in July 1984, Liverpool made far greater ones. It dropped many of its spending plans and did a lot of creative accounting. It first reorganised the accounts for 1983/84 to reduce the deficit that was being carried into 1984/85, as table 2 shows. Over £m3 was deducted from the 1983/84 budget because the treasurer had overprovided for inflation. Labour used £m4 of its reserves to reduce the deficit in 1983/84. It also adopted the Government's suggestion on the method of repaying interest charges on loans. This saved £m2.6 in 1983/84 although it meant more would be paid in the longer term. Most important, Tony Byrne agreed to 'capitalise' housing repairs rather than putting them on the revenue budget. This further reduced the deficit by £m5. Expenditure in 1983/84 was retrospectively reduced from £m231 to £m218, and the city avoided the £m17 in grant penalties. The deficit carried into 1984/85 was reduced from a threatened £m34 to £m4.7 (see table 2).

Table 2: How the 1983/84 Budget Deficit was Reduced

		£m
Total deficit reduction		30.0
Lower rate of inflation	–	3.1
The use of reserves	–	4.0
Debt rescheduling	–	2.6
Capitilising housing repairs	–	5.0
Additional growth items cost	+	1.2
Penalty for overspending	–	16.5

The deficit was reduced by £m30 from £m34.7 to £m4.7

Having reduced the deficit for 1983/84, Byrne then reduced the 1984/85 budget from £m262 to £m223, as table 3 shows. Inflation of pay and prices had been less than anticipated in 1983/84, so the base budget in 1984/85 was reduced by £m3.8 to allow for this. Rescheduling the repayment of debts in 1984/85 also saved £m2.9. But these were accounting matters. The major savings were made by cancelling nearly all of Labour's new policies. The decoration allowances were simply abandoned, reducing expenditure by £m8.5. Housing repairs were again put on the capital budget. This saved a further £m8.6 in 1984/85.

The money that had been intended to cover existing, but unacknowledged service commitments, was also dropped from the July budget. No specific provision was made for the £m4.3 unallocated reductions originally proposed by the Liberals in their 1983/84 budget. Similarly, no provision was made for the cost of 350 staff actually on the payroll, but not included in the city's base budget, which had been priced at £m3 in the deficit budget. Finally, the deficit budget had set aside £m3.4 to pay for continuing employment on Manpower Service Commission schemes. This was reduced to £m1.3 in July. Labour's July budget assumed that the money needed to finance this spending would be found from the contingency fund or by economies during the year or it would lead to overspending.

The original deficit budget had provided £m8 to cover for contingen-

Table 3: How the 1984/85 Budget Total was Reduced

		£m
Budget reduction		39.3
Lower rate of inflation	−	3.8
Debt rescheduling	−	2.9
Capitalising housing repairs	−	8.6
Increased government grants	−	8.1
Decoration allowance dropped	−	8.5
Unallocated reductions not covered	−	4.3
Existing staff salaries not covered	−	3.0
Reduction in salary cover MSC employees	−	2.1
Reductions in committee expenditure	−	2.0
Contingency fund increased by	+	4.0

Original deficit budget reduced from £m262 to £m223.

cies and inflation. This was increased by £m4 in the July budget to provide for all the unallocated savings, extra staff and the Manpower Service Commission employees. However, this was wildly optimistic since in the original budget they had been costed at £m9.6. On top of these changes, Labour was able to add the extra £m8.6 it had got from the Government. When they were added up, the 1984/85 budget was reduced by over £m39 to £m223. This was close enough to the Government's target so that the authority would not pay any penalties. And the rate rise was reduced from over 170 per cent to 17 per cent.

The question was who, if anyone, had won? The deal had been achieved by a variety of creative accounting techniques which could not necessarily be repeated in future years. Labour did gain some concessions from the Government with its bankruptcy threats. But it had to drop many of its plans and postpone difficult choices for following years. If the city used in 1984/85 the £m7 reserves it had planned to save for future use, it would need a 45 per cent rate increase the next year just to cover for them. Yet the city had used them. Amid the political furore, neither side had any interest in making plain this kind of elementary fact.

The deal left open the question whether the city could pay for its services without making cuts later in the year or running up a large deficit. But it would be difficult for the Labour leadership to sell any cuts to its own supporters in the council group and the district Labour party. Labour's July budget resembled those of its Liberal predecessors. For many years budgets in Liverpool had been exercises in heroic assumptions which failed to be met. They were expressions of intent more or less consciously pursued, but frequently never arrived at. As the city treasurer admitted, if the April 'deficit' budget had been a very pessimistic one, the July 'legal' budget had been equally optimistic.

Each side made the wrong claims. Liverpool's long-term financial problems were greater than the Government was willing to admit. It also knew that many of the measures it wanted the city to adopt in the short term, would store up problems in the longer-term. But it had no wish to publicise this. It simply wanted to get the show on the road. The Labour group was equally anxious to publicise the political concessions it had got from the Government. This prevented it exploiting as much as possible the larger financial problems it would continue to face. Also the Labour council could not present a rate increase much greater than 17 per cent without losing face with the electorate. It certainly could not have got a much larger one through the district Labour party. Yet the rate rise should have been much greater to balance the books. While outsiders might have heaved a collective sigh of relief at the apparent settlement, those on the inside well understood that 1984 was a prelude to further struggles in 1985.

'Positive progress' on housing

The real key to getting agreement on a legal budget in 1984 was Liverpool's housing programme. Tony Byrne's refusal to capitalise two years' housing repairs provoked the budget crisis. His final decision to do so, resolved it. His move during the June meetings with Jenkin to look beyond the 1984/85 budget to the longer-term question of housing resources for the city was a key event in the whole battle. But to get him to do this the Government had to offer a quid pro quo. This was again spelt out in the letter to John Hamilton in which Jenkin agreed with the Labour party about the importance of future money for Liverpool's housing programme. 'I well understand,' Jenkin wrote, 'that a decision by your council to allow capitalisation of expenditure previously charged to revenue, thereby easing revenue commitments in 1984/85, will be influenced by the effect this might have on your capital resources in future years.' That is, if the city used its capital allowance to repair existing homes, it would have less money with which to build new houses. And Jenkin accepted that there was 'no disagreement between us about the scale of the problems you face.'

On the other hand, Jenkin also argued 'we agree that improving the quality of management and maintenance is essential if better value is to be secured for the substantial sums of money spent.' Not only the authority's resources, but those of the private sector, and 'the enthusiasm and resourcefulness of the housing associations and the local community groups you serve, are also there to be tapped.' In other words, the Government believed that the city's housing problems were caused not merely by lack of cash, but by management and policy failures within the authority itself. Nevertheless, the Government was anxious to see how its resources could help deal with the problem and develop 'an effective and constructive partnership to tackle the needs of the people of Liverpool.'

Patrick Jenkin wrote to John Hamilton 'I can give you an assurance that I will do my very best to ensure that allocations to Liverpool next year under the housing investment programme and the urban programme, taken together, will enable the council to make positive progress in dealing with the city's severe needs, having regard to the scale of your capital commitments and the resources (including possible proceeds of sales of council dwellings and freeholds) available to you.' In other words, he implied that if Liverpool would balance its budget for 1984/85 by using its housing allowance to pay for repairs, he would at least make sure it would not restrict its ability to build new housing next year.

No sum of money was attached to the offer. It was conditional on Labour diversifying its housing strategy. But the offer was clearly made. These 'understandings' about future treatment were a crucial factor in Byrne's decision to abandon the deficit budget. At the July budget meeting, he turned to the Government representative, Eric Sorenson, and publicly reminded him of the promises Patrick Jenkin had made about money for housing. He warned him that if those promises were not kept, he would take the expenditure on housing repairs out of the capital account back into revenue and immediately create a financial crisis that year. The appalled official realised that Byrne might never let the Government off the hook. This argument about Liverpool's housing problems, and the extent and nature of the help the Government had offered, continued long beyond July 1984.

For the time being the issue was settled. But the things which the council had to do to balance the books, and Derek Hatton's exploitation of the victory, guaranteed that the resolution would be a temporary one. The basic financial problem had been avoided and a lot of political hostages to fortune had been given. The 'understandings' on which the deal was made were very fragile. Liverpool's budget saga had a long way further to go. It would require a lot of goodwill on the part of both sides if there was to be a peaceful resolution in the next round. The circumstances were not promising. The spectre of Labour leaders 'dancing on the grave' of Patrick Jenkin in 1984 would return to haunt them in 1985.

MONEY, POLITICS AND HOUSING: WORSENING CONFLICT – July 1984 - May 1985

6

By the time Liverpool had settled its quarrel with the Government in July 1984, it was already four months into the financial year. And the Government had almost prepared its plans for local government spending for the next financial year 1985/86. This meant that the two years virtually ran into each other without any political respite. Between the summer of 1984 and the spring of 1985, Liverpool's Labour party and the Government got locked into a further series of disputes which drove the wedge between the two sides deeper than ever.

During these months relations eventually deteriorated so much that Patrick Jenkin and his officials finally refused to talk to the city about its budget problems any more, bluntly telling Labour to stop complaining and get on with sorting out their financial affairs. The Government claimed it had been willing in July to help ease Liverpool through its financial crisis with some special cash, if it would play the game. In the end they simply gave up because Labour would not cooperate. Labour politicians denied any substantial help was ever offered by the Government after July. As one of the central union figures said about their hints of offers 'They would say that, wouldn't they . . .' It can never be certain what offer the Government would have made, what the conditions might have been and whether it would have been big enough to make a difference to the city's financial problems. There remains a critical question mark lingering over the whole affair.

Whoever was right, the breakdown in communications became crucial in the summer of 1985 when, after a further year of unexpected twists and turns in the saga, the whole thing seemed to go wrong for Labour. The inability, or unwillingness, of each side to negotiate was partly responsible for the fact that the Liverpool Labour party finally toppled over the edge of the financial and political precipice it had walked along for almost two years. For much of the second year of the conflict, it seemed that Labour would walk to safety beyond the edge. Instead, the party became the unintended victim of its own campaign against the Government as it finally slid down the side of the precipice towards municipal bankruptcy.

The lessons of 1984

The two sides had drawn very different conclusions from the events of 1984. But another confrontation in 1985 was made virtually inevitable. The Government realised it had made a tactical error in being drawn into prolonged negotiations with Liverpool, which had only brought it trouble with its friends and its enemies. It also recognised it had lost the propaganda battle in 1984, and had failed to get its arguments across to the electorate. The Government now decided to shift the ground of the argument and attack the Labour council directly in future, portraying the conflict not as a technical dispute about money and grant systems, but as a Militant plot against the Government.

Liverpool, on the other hand, drew the opposite moral. It decided to exactly repeat its behaviour the following year. In the first place, its budget problems had not been resolved, merely postponed, by the July 1984 settlement. It knew it would have to return to the financial argument with the Government. It also wanted to repeat its political victory. The Liverpool Labour party very successfully exploited its modest gains to claim enormous political credit with other Labour authorities. After July everybody wanted to know how Liverpool had done this, and the city sent a steady stream of speakers across the country publicising its achievements.

Liverpool, and Derek Hatton in particular, made the running at the Labour Party's annual conference in November 1984 and, much to the unease of the national leadership, got the national party committed to support Labour local authorities who resisted the law in defence of essential jobs and services. This strengthened the resolve of the resisting rate-capped authorities. Liverpool badly wanted to keep going the momentum of that political struggle with the Conservative Government, as well as force the national Labour Party further to the left on the issue. It was especially important to the Militants in Liverpool to continue the fight. The bloody nose which Derek Hatton claimed to have given Margaret Thatcher with the victory in July, was a perfect advert for what a hard left party could do when it stood up to the Government. Militant, who had ambitions to play on a broader national stage, used it as an important platform for its recruitment campaign across the country.

The July success also reinforced the position of its principal architect, Tony Byrne. In future, it became difficult to challenge his arguments, since no one else in the party had mastered the intricacies of the city's finances. Even the professional officers had little influence over Byrne's policies. In 1984, as one officer put it, Byrne played a game of cat and mouse with Patrick Jenkin. Once the Minister walked into the trap, Byrne pulled down the gate and Jenkin could not escape. Byrne also knew the game had to be played again in 1985. The other councillors trusted him to do it. When later in 1984 the treasurer's report pointed out the seriousness of the city's financial position, one councillor simply said 'Tony got us out of the mess last year and he will do it again this year.' That remained an open question.

Hostilities resumed : free market conservatism versus 'municipal Stalinism.'

The second round of the conflict opened almost as soon as the first ended. The mutual recriminations over the budget had hardly settled, when hostilities broke out again. In late July the Government announced Liverpool's spending target for 1985/86. It was set at £m222, an increase of £m6 over 1984–85, but in real terms a decrease. John Hamilton was 'shocked and disappointed' claiming that unless there was a change in the settlement 'we will be back at square one and challenging him again next year.' In a supreme piece of unintended irony, Hamilton argued 'Jenkin has learnt nothing from the Liverpool experience.'

Nothing could be further from the truth. Patrick Jenkin had learned his lesson well and had prepared a new tough line. The Government would not single Liverpool out for special treatment next year – there would be 'no soft options.' The answer to its difficulties was not more Government money but 'vigorous policies to root out inefficiency in their service provision.' Jenkin gradually began to implement his new strategy – broadening the Government's attack on the Labour council, emphasing its 'municipal Stalinism', its ideological isolation from other Labour authorities, and its conflicts with many people within the city.

Underlining this new-found toughness, Jenkin warned other Labour authorities 'If anyone thinks they are going to get something by aping the antics of Liverpool in going to the brink of bankruptcy they have got another think coming.' Attitudes had already hardened by the autumn of 1984 and even during the preliminary skirmishes, did not bode well for the next round. But neither Liverpool nor the other authorities believed the Government's tougher line would be held.

Relations between Liverpool and the Government deteriorated through the autumn. In September, Kenneth Baker was drafted into the Department of the Environment as Minister for Local Government, to give it more backbone in its struggles with other Labour authorities. It was announced that Patrick Jenkin would now have more time to spend in Liverpool and was hoping to improve relations with the Labour council through regular direct contacts. It was hinted that increased urban aid money might be available if the council cooperated. However, as one of his advisers pointed out 'We have got to try to find areas where dialogue can take place with the city council. Patrick Jenkin will be trying. But it takes two to tango.' The city did not want to dance. There were constant wranglings about the details of all Labour's dealings with the Government – the July budget settlement, the city's housing programme, the management of its urban programme.

Eventually the Government became tired of having its tail twisted by Liverpool and decided to go on the offensive. In October 1984 Jenkin launched an ideological broadside on the Labour leadership who he argued 'spend their entire time abusing one, attacking and criticising. They can't expect us to put up with it forever.' Invoking the outside world against Liverpool, he argued it was 'increasingly difficult for me to sell the need for substantial additional help for Liverpool when all they do is turn round and kick us in the teeth.' He would try to defend what he was doing for the city but 'there comes a point when people say "Look, why are you wasting your time and our money on an unappreciative part of the country?".'

Jenkin argued the city was being run in an unacceptable way. In particular, the professional officers had been excluded from decision-making. In many cases 'they simply don't know what's happening. They aren't told.' But nor was anyone else in his view. The centralisation of power meant that Liverpool 'was being handled by a few leading councillors.' Jenkin claimed this was not just a matter of political differences between them and the Government, because they had quite effective working relationships with other left-wing councils. Jenkin had begun to focus on an issue which had always worried the national Labour party – the secretiveness with which party policy was made and the role in it of the influential Militant Tendency, through its interlocking membership of the district Labour party, its powerful executive committee and the Labour group.

The dispute between the two was about more than style. It was essentially a conflict of ideologies. The Thatcher free market Government was very unhappy with Liverpool's rejection of the Conservative strategy for the revival of the city – private-sector-led economic revival – and its adoption of a 'total municipal solution.' Jenkin argued that the Labour council was excluding the private sector, housing associations, and housing co-operatives from its housing strategy, instead concentrating all of its financial and housing resources in a limited number of places in the city 'to the exclusion of all else.' He was sceptical of Liverpool's own plan for revival, its urban regeneration strategy, which was fundamentally 'unbalanced' in trying to revive the local economy solely through a council house building programme which ignored the need to help small businesses. The Government was equally unhappy with the Labour council's efforts to 'municipalise' community and voluntary provision in the city, either by wholly taking over projects which had previously been supported by the council, or stopping their funding altogether. Jenkin was not only expressing the Government's disapproval of a left-wing Labour authority. He was trying to encourage and capitalise upon some local concern about the ideological thrust and political style of the Labour council.

Financial worries again

These ideological differences between the hard-right Thatcher administration and the hard-left city council were a central part of the the conflict between the two sides. However, in November 1984 another threatening issue arose, which dominated relations between the two sides during the next four months, and led the Government along another tortuous path. It was not directly concerned with Liverpool's long-running revenue problems but with the money for its housing programme, the city's capital budget. The revenue budget paid for all the services the city provided on an annual basis and was financed by rates, rents and government grants. The capital budget paid for long-term construction and was financed by borrowing. Eventually, of course, the loans had to be repaid from the city's revenue budget.

Although the council finally paid for the work, the Government could decide how much construction the city could carry out, by setting a limit on what it could borrow and on the proportion of its own assets it could use to to pay for the work. In Liverpool almost 85 per cent of its capital budget was used for housing. The money it could spend on this in 1985/86 had been a key element in the July settlement. As the Government had always feared, the new dispute in November stemmed from the terms of that settlement. A central part of the July deal had been Byrne's decision to balance the budget by 'capitalising' two years' housing repairs, over £m13. He only agreed to do this because Patrick Jenkin promised that he would do all he could the following year to help ease Liverpool's housing problems. The issue exploded in the face of the Government, ironically, on 5 November, Guy Fawkes night.

That day civil servants from the Task Force met councillors and local officers in a routine meeting to discuss the city's housing programme for 1985/86. But the meeting had to be abandoned when Tony Byrne refused to carry on until the civil servants gave him a guarantee that the Government would allow Liverpool a capital budget of £m130 in 1985/86 to carry out its massive council house building programme. Byrne insisted Jenkin had promised this in July 1984. The alarmed civil servants promptly denied any such promises had been made, pulling out of a briefcase as evidence a copy of the 29 June letter to John Hamilton from Patrick Jenkin, as well as a transcript they had kept of the crucial 9 July meeting in London. But the claim sent the civil servants dashing back to talk to the Minister to establish a sensible response to this new demand from their difficult opponent.

Eleven days later, in a letter to the chief executive, Alfred Stocks, the Task Force insisted that Jenkin's 'own recollections' as well as the official record confirmed the Minister had 'made no such promise' and that 'no reasonable interpretation of anything said then could support your allegation.' The letter also underlined that Jenkin had emphasised several times during the discussions in July that no firm commitment could be given for 1985/86. It also insisted that the offer of help had been made only if Liverpool would broaden its housing strategy by diluting its municipalisation programme and pulling in the private and voluntary sectors.

Byrne refused to back down arguing that the Government had reneged on the promise of £m130 it had made in July. 'We would not have agreed to make a budget without that promise' he said. Patrick Jenkin had told 'deliberate and calculated lies.' Kenneth Baker angrily denied any such promise had been made. The council had made 'a new and totally false claim.' The figure was three times this year's allocation, and belonged 'in cloud cuckoo land. No responsible council could possibly base its plans on such a wild assumption.'

The issue spilled out onto the front pages of the national press when the Government released the transcript of the 9 July discussions. In answer to Byrne's claim that Liverpool needed a £m130 capital programme, Jenkin said 'there is nothing I can do except take note of what you say.' He hoped 'to encourage positive progress in dealing with the housing problem. I cannot go further than say it would be our aim to do this . . . what I cannot do is to give some kind of quantified undertaking.' Byrne's eliptical reply, however, was 'We don't need you to say yes. It is sufficient that you don't say no. In fact we would rather you didn't say yes. They are simple folk in the party who are only interested in the programmes. We need to indicate to the party that we would be in a position to carry out that scale of progress, which is the minimum needed.'

The conversation could hardly be described as a firm foundation on which Liverpool should base a major new housing programme. But there was enough in the exchange, when combined with the 'admitted offer' in the original letter from Patrick Jenkin to John Hamilton, to let Labour make a lot of political capital from its claim that the Government had broken the spirit of the summer's agreement, when Jenkin had publicly admitted the scale of Liverpool's housing problems. This was particularly true when, in December, as part of a national cut in housing expenditure, the Government actually cut Liverpool's housing funds for 1985/86 by almost 20 per cent. Labour then was able to claim the Government was being especially punitive against Liverpool because of the way it had exploited politically the July budget settlement.

The Government argued that Liverpool had refused to read the very obvious signal it had given them in July – that they would get extra resources for housing only if they would play ball. Although it would never have trebled its housing allocation, in July 1984 the Government claimed to be willing to provide more money for Liverpool the following year. It was only because of Labour's intransigence on its municipal housing strategy that the cuts in its housing budget were made. The approximate amount that was taken from the Labour council's housing budget, £m9, was later added to the Housing Corporation's budget for housing in Liverpool, to promote the work of housing associations and diversify housing provision in the city.

In other words, what the Government was unable to make Liverpool do indirectly, it decided to get done directly through its own quango. If the Labour council would not cooperate and spend its money on the kind of mixed-economy housing programme the Government wanted, it would give it to someone else who would. Only three months after the Government believed it had offered an olive branch to the Labour council, it had been spurned. In its view, the Labour council had exploited the July settlement and was now trying to embarrass Jenkin and the Government once again, by misrepresenting what they had said at the time. But for Byrne this was not a political game. He had decided what he wanted – a big public housing programme – and believed what he said about the Government. In his eyes they had reneged.

Politics and housing in Liverpool

This dispute about housing was central to the ideological battle between the the Government and the Labour council, as well as to Liverpool politics. In the 1970s and the early 1980s, the Liberals, anticipating current conservative philosophy, had encouraged the private and voluntary sector in housing at the expense of the public sector, and had abandoned council house building. That policy had provoked great bitterness at the time and Labour came into office determined to reverse the process and to develop a massive public housing programme virtually at all costs. Tony Byrne was the architect of this policy termed the urban regeneration strategy. This combined the resources of the housing programme and the urban programme, which the Liberals had concentrated on grants to small businesses and environmental improvement schemes. Labour channelled all the money into 17 priority areas in the city providing housing, parks and sports centres.

The Labour council claimed that this was the largest public housing programme in the country which would build more council houses in a single year than all other local authorities put together. Between 1983 and 1986 the programme would both provide 6,000 homes and, by stimulating the local economy through the construction industry, would create 16,000 jobs. But the programme was controversial. Critics argued that although Liverpool's housing need was great, with 22,000 sub-standard houses and 20,000 people on the waiting list, the policy had many weaknesses – the pace of change was too dramatic; it was bulldozing too many recoverable properties; it neglected too many other areas of the city; it neglected community and residential preferences; it provided too much architecturally anonymous, low-rise family housing in the inner city when the need was for more diverse provision for a range of client groups; it was too centralised; it could not be properly managed by the housing department and it would eventually lead to low-rise slums in the 1990s as opposed to the high-rise slums of the 1960s.

Tony Byrne's response was that the scale of need and dereliction of Liverpool's housing was so great, that only a centralised policy could deal with the problem. Since Labour might only control the city for a short time, the programme had to be rapidly implemented. Because resources were limited, they had to be concentrated in public housing. More to the point was Byrne's ideological defence of the programme. 'I am a Socialist,' he once said 'I believe in public ownership, control and accountability for housing through the elected council. It is the local authority who must satisfy the needs of the working class. Working class organisation in this city lies in the Labour party and the unions and not in housing associations.' The mixed economy approach to housing provision currently favoured by his own national party was, in Byrne's words, 'the consensus politics that have failed.' In other words, everything the Government stood for in housing he opposed, and vice versa.

As in the budget battle itself, the dogmatism of each side reinforced their determination not to concede. It guaranteed what another Labour politician called 'the politics of the bunker.' When asked by The

Guardian newspaper whether the block-busting style of the policy might not recreate the high-rise failures of local politicians in the 1960s, Byrne's simple reply was that the problem was that all those previous politicians had been 'dickheads.' The housing programme was Byrne's passion, and his main reason for running Liverpool. And it was this which Patrick Jenkin was threatening to deny him by his refusal to increase his capital budget.

But Tony Byrne was determined to get what he wanted. He had spent several years in opposition developing his ideas and mastering the intricacies of housing policy. The housing programme was to be Labour's legacy to Liverpool. If the party could not get that, there was no point in having power. There was certainly no point in having power just to implement the Tory Government's cuts in services. In this way, the argument about the capital programme spilt over into the one about the revenue budget. This argument over housing led Byrne to re-open the argument over the July 1984 revenue budget settlement. From November 1984 onwards, the capital and the revenue budgets became inextricably tried together.

Going for bust on housing?

In November 1984 the capital programme was the more pressing issue because Liverpool had begun to act as if it was in fact going to get extra money from the Government. The council had signed contracts for house building in 1985/86 which seemed likely to outstrip the money the city would have to pay with. The amount a local authority can spend is determined mainly by what the Government allows it to borrow in its housing investment programme, combined with other smaller government grants, plus a fixed percentage of the capital receipts it receives from selling off existing assets. By December 1984 Liverpool had signed contracts for 1985/86 worth £m88, and the treasurer estimated that the city would be £m11 short of the money it needed. This would have to be found from some other source. But he did not say which. Just as six months earlier Liverpool had gambled on its high-risk, illegal revenue budget, now it was apparently doing so in its capital programme.

To make matters worse, in late December the Government announced its national housing programme for 1985/86. Major cuts in expenditure reduced the money available from £bn1.8 in 1984/85 to

£bn1.6 in 1985/86. Equally crucial, in trying to control public expenditure, the Conservatives cut the percentage of capital receipts from their council house sales that the local authorities could spend on new housing, from 40 per cent to 20 per cent. The announcement caused an uproar nationally with the local authorities, the building industry and the Labour Party. In Parliament 30 Conservative MPs abstained upon and three voted against the Government's policy.

The impact of this policy upon Liverpool was enormous. Its housing investment programme was reduced from £m46 in 1984/85 to £m37 in 1985/86. Most important, Liverpool was given a much larger cut in housing budget than every other local authority on Merseyside. Two of them received a 7 per cent cut, another 14 per cent and a fourth 17 per cent. Liverpool's cut was 20 per cent. Labour claimed that the cuts were made in a vindictive fashion against the city, as Jenkin's retribution for the trouble they had caused him in July. The capital receipts Liverpool could spend was also reduced from £m21 in 1984/85 to £m13 in 1985/86. All together it was a 34 per cent cut in housing resources and the city would not be able to pay for a housing programme which was already running at £m88. This was six months after Patrick Jenkin had promised to make positive progress to solve the city's housing problems! Byrne called it 'a declaration of war on Liverpool.'

It seemed a politically inept move by the Government – unless it was primarily interested in teaching Liverpool a lesson. In fact, it was another sign that the Government had had enough of Liverpool. It would put housing money in other local authorities on Merseyside where it got the kind of political response it wanted. Byrne was not easily put off his goal of building housing fit for Liverpool's working classes. He simply refused to accept the Government's cuts. 'We will not' he said, 'reduce our building programme by one single unit.' This seemed no idle threat when in mid-January the treasurer revealed that Liverpool had now signed contracts worth £m96. Once all its income had been added up, the city was still £m32 short of its planned expenditure. Even though the treasurer was exploring ways of raising the money, just over two months before the financial year started, the Labour council had no visible way of paying for one third of the building work for which it had signed contracts. In his anxiety to press on with the housing programme, Byrne had apparently overstretched himself.

Liverpool's new venture on the housing finance front again alarmed the Government. It did not want to get drawn into the morass of Liverpool's politics once more, but finally decided it had to move against the council before the financial and legal problems got out of hand. On 7 February the Government announced that Patrick Jenkin was considering using a little-known and previously unused power under the 1980 Local Government Act which would give him the authority to stop the Labour council spending the £m96. If the Minister used a section 78 order, after 1 April 1985, all the city's new contracts, and all spending above the Government's limit, would have to be approved by Jenkin personally. In other words, he would be controlling the city's building programme. He gave the city fourteen days to explain themselves, but he said 'Liverpool cannot make their own laws. It has made no secret of its determination to charge ahead irrespective of having the money to pay the bill. We have to act on it. There is no question I am picking on Liverpool.' Things had apparently gone wrong for Liverpool. The local Daily Post commented 'it must be very clear to Liverpool's labour chiefs that this year Mr. Jenkin is ready for them. He will not be caught this spring.'

Banque Parabas and Byrne's coup

Once again, nothing could be further from the truth. Tony Byrne had another ace up his sleeve. He played it on the very last of his fourteen days' grace. On 22 February he revealed that not merely had Liverpool been exploring ways of raising money. Earlier that month, after several months of secret negotiations, it had actually finalised a deal which would allow it to pay for the housing programme. This was with a banking syndicate headed by Banque Parabas, one of the largest French banks recently nationalised by President Mitterand's socialist administration. The deal was complicated but the principle was simple. In recent years Liverpool had sold off over 7,000 council houses and was receiving monthly payments from them on long-term mortgages. In the new deal, the city had managed to sell its interest in those mortgages to the banking syndicate, from which it would receive a lump sum of £m30 immediately. The city could then call that money a capital receipt and spend part of it on its house building programme. It seemed a perfect arrangement.

However, there was a potential problem. The banks had an escape clause which gave them the right to make Liverpool buy back all the mortgages after seven years, even though they did not in fact plan to use it. The treasurer, Michael Reddington, explained that the city could have got a deal over twenty-five years which could have avoided the problem of repurchasing. It would also have got £m2 less from the banks. He did not think it justifiable to lose that £m2 just to insure against the possibility of being forced to buy the mortgages back. This was the key issue. The Government could argue it was neither an outright disposal by the city, nor a purchase by the banks, rather a seven-year loan. In which case, the money would not be a capital receipt and the Labour council could not use the money to pay for its housing programme. The city, of course, as was increasingly common in the now highly litigious area of local government finance, had taken the advice of a QC. He had confirmed the city solicitor's view that the deal was legal. The question was what the Government would make of it.

The financial package which Labour had drawn up for Patrick Jenkin had other awkward details. If the French bank deal was allowed, the city would be able to spend £m9 of the £m30. This would increase what it had to pay for its building programme from £m64 to £m73. But on its own this would not close the gap and raise the necessary £m97. The city did this by revising the figures in two equally unusual ways, which were explained by Michael Reddington. It argued that since Liverpool had never spent as much as it planned on its capital programme, but usually underspent its total by about 10 per cent, it was reasonable to assume this 'slippage' would happen again in 1985/86. In which case, £m10 should be deducted from its planned expenditure of £m97.1.

The city then argued that although they were usually regarded as synonymous, there was an important distinction between total capital spending and what the 1980 Act called a local authority's 'prescribed expenditure', which the Government could control. Liverpool argued that capital expenditure on repairs and maintenance, as opposed to new construction, 'are not, or may not be' counted as 'prescribed expenditure.' It then claimed that in 1985/86, £m11 of its planned programme was for repairs, and this amount should be substracted from the total of 'prescribed expenditure.' It also argued that over £m1 capital expenditure, which the city got from its various leases also might not count as prescribed expenditure. When added together, these reduced the 'prescribed expenditure' in the capital programme by over £m23 from £m97 to £m73. Since its income was boosted to £m73, the Labour council argued the shortfall had been reduced from £m32 to £600,000. As it was also exploring other ways of staying within the limits – like selling other kinds of mortgages or deferring payments to builders – Labour claimed Patrick Jenkin had no grounds for taking control of the city's building programme. This was a very clever piece of creative accounting.

The deal was immediately splashed across the pages of the national press. Derek Hatton claimed that Liverpool had 'demonstrated the way to find the finance to build council houses. We hope other local authorities will follow what Liverpool has done.' Byrne rubbed Jenkin's nose in it, claiming that the Minister did not even understand the capital allocation process. 'He became gripped by his desire to seek vengeance on the people of Liverpool and didn't bother to look at the figures.' Once more Liverpool had pulled a propaganda coup over Jenkin, which brought many other Labour authorities to the city to find out how to beat the Government.

The Government was again in a difficult political dilemma. The legal position had not been tested, but it soon transpired that the Government's own lawyers had considered such a deal illegal when the idea had been floated a few years earlier. They had doubted whether a council could sell its mortgages or whether the money could be called a capital receipt. Jenkin tried to meet the Labour leaders to talk about the case. They were now quite certain of their position and refused to see him. Patrick Jenkin was 'not happy at all' with Liverpool's plan, which his lawyers were considering and he claimed it was 'doubtful whether the council has the power to do what it is suggesting.' But Jenkin changed his mind. At the end of March he announced the deal was legal after all. Liverpool's propaganda victory continued. By making his move at the very last moment, when all eyes were on the city, Tony Byrne publicly outwitted the Government. At the same time he made Jenkin seem callous in trying to cut Liverpool's housing programme after promising them extra help six months earlier. Most important, at the end of the day, Byrne still got what he wanted – the money to pay for the urban regeneration stragegy.

This was more than a mere propaganda victory. In some ways it changed the equation of Liverpool's financial politics. As Byrne constantly insisted, he was not primarily interested in a confrontation with the Government, but in getting the Labour party's policies implemented. The fact that he was now in a position to finance a further year of the building programe and produce another 1,500 council houses made it more important to him to keep control of the city in 1985/86. That affected the way he viewed the other half of the city's financial problems, the revenue budget. Even though those problems were still large, a new pressure had arisen to persuade the Labour leaders to avoid a financial collapse for as long as possible – even though they believed it was inevitable in the long run – and to avoid a confrontation with the Government in the spring of 1985.

To some extent the Government saw it in this way too. It also realised that if Byrne was denied the power to carry out his housing programme he would start threatening financial suicide once again. That political calculation, and worries about the prospect of getting enmeshed in Liverpool politics again and cutting back a badly needed housing programme, compounded the Government's uncertainty about the legality of Liverpool's plan. In the end, it chose not to engage the issue, even at the risk of encouraging other Labour authorities to copy Liverpool and breach the capital spending dam. It was still better to stay away from the place and its problems.

However, the reverberations continued. In July 1985 Patrick Jenkin announced in Parliament that no more deals like this would be allowed and he would legislate to get rid of the legal uncertainty which had forced him to allow Liverpool's plan through. Jenkin admitted that, like many others, he had been 'taken aback' by the Banque Parabas deal which transferred the mortgates, without consulting the individual borrowers concerned, to foreign banks which might not even assume the risk involved in the loan. His decision would stop a number of local authority deals in the pipeline. But the political spinoff was just as revealing. As the junior Labour spokesman on the environment, Jack Straw, attempted to defend the deal, Patrick Jenkin argued it proved 'the inherent contradictions' of the Labour leadership who 'showed their respectable face' in Parliament, but 'never fail to give aid and comfort to the wreckers who do not believe in the rule of law.' Liverpool's actions continued to embarrass their national leaders.

Reopening the revenue crisis

The money for Liverpool's housing programme had been an important underlying issue in the first round of the battle in 1984. It did not become especially visible until the final stages of the negotiations. In the second round, in 1985, however, the budget for the housing programme was inextricably linked to the revenue budget from the start. In fact, the city's underlying revenue budget problems remained the same throughout the year. But the way in which they were presented by the Labour council varied throughout the period, depending upon their political needs at the time. These were frequently shaped by the status of the arguments over the housing programme.

The worse the negotiations between the council and the Government over the housing were going, the worse the revenue problems were presented by Tony Byrne. He used the city's admittedly large financial problems as a way of putting pressure on the Government to give him what he wanted on the housing programme. At one point Byrne admitted to a housing association official that Liverpool's financial pack of cards would probably collapse one day, but by that time 'we'll be so far down the road on housing, they'll never catch up with us.' In other words, if the Government did have to take over the city when it ran out of money, it would inherit a public housing programme it could never get rid of.

The tactic first became clear after the 5 November row between the two sides about the Minister's broken promises on housing. It marked the real opening shot in Labour's 1985 campaign. In many ways, the July settlement had been an extremely optimistic statement of the city's finances which concealed many of its structural financial difficulties because of 'the understandings' about the housing programme. After the row, when Jenkin denied he had made any explicit offers of financial aid for housing, Byrne instructed the treasurer to produce a report which unpicked that settlement and present a worst case analysis of Liverpool's budget position.

That report argued that the Labour council had made many changes in its original 'deficit' budget of March 1984, in order to get a settlement in July. The report's crucial claim was 'It was clear at the time of the budget, and indeed had been spelled out in the joint report and accepted by the Secretary of State, that a number of the actions then taken served only to postpone the impact of the inherent problems, or depended for their realisation upon the outcome of the continuing discussions with central government and subsequent decisions favourable to the city.' Since Liverpool had not got what it claimed it had been promised by the Government, Byrne argued that it was now perfectly legitimate for Labour to recalculate the 1984/85 figures, and put back what in had agreed to take out of its original deficit budget. This was exactly what Byrne had publicly threatened Sorenson with in his July 1984 budget speech. The row between the two sides had been explained away on paper in July. It was a simple matter for Byrne to write it in again.

Labour had done a lot of creative accounting to cut the March deficit budget of £m262 down to £m223 in July. It continued the Liberal practice of underestimating the real costs of paying for existing services and employees, ignoring any deficit that would be accumulated by the end of the year. It also decided to use up all of its £m11 reserves. It simply ignored the problem of balancing the 1985/86 budget, when all these reserves would be gone and the city would have to increase rates by 45 per cent in 1985/86 just to make up for that £m11. It also re-scheduled the debt repayments which reduced short-term costs, but imposed greater longer-term costs. It took the cost of £m13 housing repairs out of the revenue budget, in view of the 'promises' of future help from Jenkin.

The treasurer's statement in November simply showed what would happen to the budgets if all this creative accounting were all reversed. When the real costs of paying for existing services were added back in, the 1984/85 base budget would not be £m223 but £m231. Once inflation during the year was added, the treasurer estimated the actual cost of paying for the city's services that year would not be £m23 but £m245. The major impact of all the changes would be upon the deficits. If £m11 reserves were saved for 1985/86, and the housing repairs were put back on the revenue budget, this would create a deficit in 1983/84 of £m19 and of £m45 in 1984/85. If the city continued to take on employees from Manpower Services Commission programmes, and the Government withheld urban programme money it had promised in July, with penalties this would increase the eventual deficit in 1984/85, by a further £m16. Since the treasurer had already reported in November 1984 that there was likely to be a deficit of £m14 anyway by the end of the year, this could mean that the city would start the financial year in 1985/86 with an enormous inherited deficit of £m96.

The real cost of the 1984/85 budget had been put at £m243, the starting point for the 1985/86 budget. To that figure the treasurer added the revenue costs of decisions already taken by Labour. This would increase the base budget to £m256. This could be £m265 once inflation in 1985/86 was added on. If Byrne again refused to capitalise housing repairs in 1985/86, this would worsen the problem by adding a further £m13 and give the city a base budget of £m278. The accumulated deficits of £m96 from earlier years would have to be added, and the city would have to raise £m374 in 1985/86. At that level of spending the penalties would completely wipe out any grant from the Government, and Liverpool would have to raise the rates by over 220 per cent to pay for its programmes.

These calculations were designed to put the bleakest face on Liverpool's budget problem to strengthen its hand against the Government. Some of the threats, such as reversing the capitalisation, were not likely to be carried out, and the deficits were to that extent artificially inflated. But the calculations about the real cost of the base budget were broadly accurate. In 1985/86 it might cost up to £m265 to run the city, which could require a rate rise in the region of 85 per cent. That was the scale of Labour's problem. The worst case scenario of £m374 and a 220 per cent rate rise, however, was really designed to put pressure on the Government to reopen all the larger arguments about the grant, which the city had tried to make in the 1984 'joint report.' The council again wanted its target increased, certain expenditure exempted from grant penalties, special treatment under the urban programme, and an increased capital budget to allow it to keep a major housing programme going.

However, these demands had the reverse effect upon the Government. After this it decided it was pointless to try to talk about the grant with Liverpool. Jenkin and his officials refused to have any further discussion about Liverpool's budget problems after November 1984. This virtually marked the end of any contact between the Government and the Labour council about its financial problems. By November 1984, Patrick Jenkin had realised that the Labour group would never stop making their argument about their financial problems. He was not prepared to solve those problems for them. There was no point continuing the discussions if Liverpool was only going to try to make political capital out of them. But the city's financial problems did not go away. They remained very large indeed.

Massaging the overdraft

By this time the problem of the two financial years had become deeply entwined. The size of any budget problem in 1985/86 was obviously going to be affected by the way the 1984/85 budget turned out, especially by how much it was overspent. The precise state of Liverpool's revenue budget in 1984/85 varied enormously throughout the year. And again it reflected the state of relations with the Government, as well as the political needs of the council. These changed during the year. The city's spending seemed in order at the beginning of the financial year, deteriorated alarmingly in the middle, but appeared to be brought back under much more control by the end of the financial year 1984/85.

In the first months after July, the treasurer implied the city was broadly on target for the £m223 figure. Gradually it became clear that the optimistic assumptions made in the July budget were not going to be met. By October the treasurer indicated that the city would need to spend £m227, with penalties this would cause a deficit at the end of the year of £m14. In December the position was worse, with a predicted overall deficit of £m17. And of course the city by this time had reported a potential deficit of £m11 on its capital programme. By January 1985, three months from the end of the financial year, the treasurer was predicting a deficit of £m25. The deficit on the capital housing programme was now up to £m32. Liverpool's finances appeared to be quite out of control.

In February there had been little change in spending. However the predicted deficit for the year was reduced to £m20 by some creative accounting. But by March the pattern had changed dramatically. The deficit had been cut in half to £m10. It had been achieved primarily by combing all sources of possible income for the city, which had produced an extra £m3. Just as marginal overspending produced large penalties earlier in the year, marginal reductions produced a correspondingly large drop in penalty of over £m6, and a halving of the deficit. Almost half of the saving was accounted for by an increase in housing subsidy from the Government – the result of months of assiduous examination of complicated records of building programmes over a period of years, to discover where subsidies had been missed in the past.

This no longer seemed like the actions of a city bent on financial suicide. In the last part of the financial year, the Labour council had been trying very hard to get a grip on its finances. Projected overspending had been reduced in the previous two months by creative accounting and by maximising income from a variety of sources. In the final month, in an effort to get political control over the usual bureaucratic rush to use up remaining departmental budgets before the end of the financial year, Tony Byrne had instructed officials that no new money could be spent on anything in the authority, except what was absolutely necessary to pay for existing commitments. The result was that the city's overspending was reduced from a threatened £m96 in November, to a projected high of £m25 in January, to an actual £m5 at the end of March.

If the larger financial problems remained, considerable efforts had been made to put the best gloss upon them politically. This would give the Labour leadership maximum political flexibility in presenting a budget for the next financial year to the district Labour party and the trade unions. The leaders' line on financial confrontation appeared to have softened. The local belief was that, especially after Byrne had won his victory over Patrick Jenkin in March to keep the housing programme going, the incentive for the party to remain in power and press on with its policies was pushing it toward a compromise. The question was whether it wanted a compromise, and if it did, would its financial problems, despite recent massaging, give it enough political space to make one?

The March 1985 'no rates' budget

In the spring of 1985, Liverpool's position was complicated by the fact that it had joined with other authorities in a national campaign against the Government's rate-capping legislation, which gave Patrick Jenkin the power to limit the expenditure of 'high spending' Labour authorities. Ironically, despite its financial quarrel with the Government, Liverpool was not regarded as serious an over-spender as others, and had not been rate-capped. But it brought its budget day forward to 7 March to keep in step with the concerted action and, like the rest of the group, moved a 'no rates' policy. There were no detailed figures just the bald statement that since the city would need to spend £m265, and its target was only £m222, 'it will be impossible to set a rate.'

The noisy and emotional budget meeting went over much familiar ground. Byrne insisted he would make no cuts in Labour's programmes. If Thatcher wanted to make the cuts, she would make them herself through her commissioners. In view of popular support for Labour in the city, Byrne argued, 'I'd rather them than me.' Virtually the last line of his speech was addressed not to the Government, but to 'the Labour Party of Kinnock, Straw and Cunningham.' It was to demand a guarantee that a future Labour Government would give an immediate amnesty to any Labour councillor disqualified from office for resisting the Tories and defending local democracy. If rhetoric were a good guide to action the leaders had already decided what their fate was to be. However, many people in the city still suspected it was not, and that Labour was bluffing.

After the 7 March meeting a curious lull lay over the budget deliberations in Liverpool as the council had to wait for moves elsewhere on the rate capping front for the next three months. Ironically, as a result of the 1984 settlement, when the city had set the rate and started getting its monthly instalments from rate payers much later in the year than usual, Liverpool had no apparent reason to move at the time. Rate income from 1984/85 was still coming into the treasurery in April and May 1985/86. The council had no need to set a rate to get income until the beginning of June. This put them in a different position from other authorities opposing Government policies and appeared to give them some freedom of movement politically. It also misled them in an important way.

The district auditor steps in

The first day of June became a crucial date in the story for another reason. Liverpool's budget crisis had always been monitored by Leslie Stanford, the district auditor, the official with the responsibility of making sure the local authority's financial affairs were in order. Stanford had written to the councillors several times since April 1984, warning them of the dangers they were in. However, the Labour leaders never took his threats seriously. In fact some Labour councillors did not even bother to open his letters. Partly they did not understand the auditor's position. They believed that he was not an independent official but Patrick Jenkin's poodle, who would not act against them until told to do so. For much of the period they thought the Government would be reluctant to push Liverpool over the brink and the district auditor was bluffing. Paradoxically, the position was quite the reverse. But it had the same delaying effect. The problem for district auditors is precisely that they are not controlled by Ministers, but independent. They are left to decide when a council is breaking the law. That is not always absolutely clear.

District auditors' duties and powers were written in a rather less controversial era. Their primary function is to certify and encourage sound accounting practices, not to enter into the highly charged area of grant politics. As a result, their powers are looser than might be assumed – loose enough for them to deliberate a long time before taking action leading to the wholesale bankruptcy of elected councillors. In 1985, the district auditor was in a difficult position as he considered when would be the right time to act against recalcitrant Liverpool. In 1984, the Labour council argued that they would get concessions from the Government by refusing to set a rate, and this was not 'wilful misconduct.' The district auditor at that time knew he would have some difficulty disproving this.

Similarly, even though the Labour council had to pay about £m1 in interest charges on the money it had borrowed in 1984 because of the delay in setting a rate, it argued that it had received an extra £m8 from the Government as a result of its actions, which was a gain not a loss. Of course in 1985, as the authority's senior officers had pointed out in their written advice to the councillors in April 1985, the position was different because the Government was not negotiating with Liverpool about its grant.

Whatever the real position, Labour believed the district auditor was a paper tiger. His warning letters to them were never very threatening. Indeed the letter he wrote to the council in April 1985 urging them to make a rate, revealed a certain degree of sympathy with it, saying 'I realise the problems facing the council especially in bringing spending plans into line with available resources. This will be difficult in the short-term, but the council will also need to be mindful of the longer-term issues; short-term expediencies may only serve to exacerbate problems later.' Until May 1985 the district auditor never gave Liverpool a deadline for setting a rate.

However, at this time another district auditor took charge of Liverpool's region. The new official, Tim McMahon, came with a reputation for toughness. The policy changed immediately. On 21 May he wrote to every councillor explaining that he was not going to rehearse the arguments of his predecessor again. He did not have to wait until the financial year was closed. He gave them until 1 June to make a rate, or he would take action against them. In fact, it was not pressure from Patrick Jenkin which made the district auditor act. He had no contact with the Government, whatever the Labour councillors thought. Finally, professional self-respect would not allow the auditor to ignore the council's constant refusal to treat seriously his powers and responsibilities, while at the same time apparently incurring losses and breaking the law. He had to choose a deadline for action and stick to it. But his timing was fateful. Tony Byrne replied there was no question that Liverpool would set a rate by 1 June. Another twist in the story had taken place. The political equation would never be the same again.

At the beginning of June 1985, the Labour council was again on the brink of a financial abyss. It had gone through another year of bitter political conflict with the Conservative Government over money and housing. It had managed, despite the Government's efforts, to accumulate a lot of money to pay for a major council house building programme. It had gained some propaganda victories along the way. It believed that it had kept its promises to the electorate. Labour had not put up the council rents, had restricted the rate rise, had protected council jobs and had built public housing for rent.

However, it had done this by confrontation rather than cooperation, because its Militant leaders believed that was the only way in which a Conservative Government could be moved. The city's longer-term financial problems had not been eased. They had been massaged throughout the year, but the city had carried forward a substantial deficit. Its base budget had slowly been expanded rather than reduced. The council was locked into a faltering campaign with other authorities against the Government, still pursuing its high risk strategy. The national Labour Party was keeping its distance. The district auditor had finally made a very serious move against them. In all of this, it had alienated the Government and dissipated its alleged goodwill towards the council. In July 1984 relations between the two had been strained. By June 1985 they were virtually ruptured. There was little prospect of help from that quarter. June would be another decisive month.

7

POLITICS AND PRESSURE FOR THE LABOUR COUNCIL – June - September 1985

Throughout 1985 there had been constant speculation about what the Labour council really wanted to do and how it would eventually resolve its political dilemma. By the spring, many civil servants, council officials, union leaders and politicians believed that the Labour group wanted a compromise and would make some kind of 'fudged' budget. The difficulty was that the group's own propaganda campaign over the previous eighteen months persuaded people that the city's financial problems were unmanageable. In 1984, they had been able to conceal many of the problems and claim a major victory over the Government. In 1985, if they could not put forward the same argument, they would have to deny the crisis was as serious as they had claimed, or take some fairly harsh measures to balance the books or carry out their threat of suicide. In the end they had to carry out that threat.

Starting to govern

There was plenty of evidence in 1985 that the Labour council was interested in retaining power and running the city. While the public confrontation over the budget was going on, the council was trying to manage the authority more efficiently. It was reorganising secondary schools; planning to rationalise further education; beginning to reorganise housing management and the direct labour organisation; talking with the unions about rationalising refuse collection; and carrying out an urban regeneration strategy. In short, a Labour council was finally facing up to Liverpool's difficulties which had been identified by the Government in the 'joint report.'

In May 1985, the council reorganised the committee system and created a new finance and strategy committee chaired by Tony Byrne to control all the authority's strategic and expenditure decision; an industrial relations committee to deal with employment and personnel issues; and a reorganised environmental services committee to look after the blue-collar workforce, especially in the refuse collection service. These changes led to opposition allegations that control of council affairs was being even more concentrated in the hands of the leading councillors – Byrne, Hatton and Mulhearn. However, they did reflect the council's most urgent managerial priorities and strengthened their ability to get a grip on the slackness which had developed in parts of the authority's management system. None of this seemed like the action of a party about to commit financial suicide.

Conflicting pressures on the council

But at the same time the Labour leadership was under conflicting political pressures – from the Government, national Militant headquarters, the local authority unions, the district Labour party, the local electorate, the black community, and the other Labour authorities in the national campaign against rate-capping. The leaders' position had been much simpler in 1984 when they faced the Government on their own, exploited the general uncertainty, and did very much what they wanted. But everybody had learned something from 1984. In June 1985 Liverpool's leaders could not pick their way through this political minefield.

The Government had learned its lesson from giving in to blackmail in 1984. It adopted a much tougher line in 1985. Jenkin and Thatcher had been furious about the way Hatton and the others had capitalised on the Government's offer of an olive branch in July 1984. This, and personal slights towards her made at later meetings, convinced Thatcher that 'they do not have enough respect for my office.' In her famous phrase, which the Labour leaders never forgot, she said 'these people must be put down.' Personally and politically she detested the Militant Liverpool leaders. They hated her. Tony Byrne, on a public platform, said of Margaret Thatcher 'she is evil personified.'

In the spring of 1985, the Government refused to talk to or negotiate with Liverpool. It similarly refused to deal with the rate-capped authorities, hastening the eventual collapse of their campaign. This meant that when Liverpool's Labour leadership was thinking of postponing the confrontation and needed some concessions from the Government to sell to its supporters as a victory, that escape route had been sealed off. In 1984, the Government had slightly lost its nerve; ironically, a year later, it decided that Liverpool was bluffing and there was no need to make any overtures. The Government could sit back and wait until Labour gave in, or its majority on the council disintegrated and some other faction emerged to run the city and take the necessary hard financial decisions to get its house in order.

The national Militant leadership in London also played its part in the struggle, with the influence it exercised in the local Labour party through Derek Hatton and two other key figures, the chairman, Tony Mulhearn, and the party's press officer, Terry Harrison, both of whom had been founder members of Militant, and were independent powerful forces in the national organisation. There were always two conflicting dimensions to national Militant's view of Liverpool. On the one hand they could see political potential in public disorder. If the local authority's services collapsed and the Government took over the city, those disorders could be used to discredit the Government as the last gasp of capitalism. This might boost Militant's recruitment. At the same time, since Liverpool was their 'jewel in the crown' it was also important for them to be seen running the city efficiently and scoring propaganda victories over Thatcher. In this way they could present Liverpool as the model working class state, a kind of socialism in one city.

The first view would lead towards outright defiance of the Government, the second towards a negotiated retreat. In 1984, the first was always a slight temptation for Militant. But the propaganda success of the July budget victory reinforced what was always the dominant strand, and by 1985 the national Militant line was much more in favour of keeping control of the city. The setbacks they were having across the country, especially their failure to gain any victories in the Labour Party's reselection of MPs, emphasised the dangers to them of being associated with chaos in Liverpool. They needed to protect their home base. On the other hand some rank-and-file Militants in Liverpool saw the issue differently. In their view, Militant would benefit if the Government resisted and there was trouble in the city, or if the Government gave in and the council scored a further propaganda victory. But they saw no benefit for Militant if the council gave in. These differences of opinion between the national and local leaders and their rank-and-file also played a crucial part in the denouement of the crisis in

June 1985. The inability of the Militant leaders to control their members led them towards illegality.

The Labour leaders would also have to sell any budget to both the district Labour party and the trade unions, neither of whom would let them get away lightly with harsh measures. Although Militant could normally organise support in the district party, this might not be automatic for a fudged deal. In 1984 many members of the district party had thought a 17 per cent rate increase was too much of a retreat. They accepted it then because of the council's apparent gains from the Government. Also, since many Militants were local authority workers, they would not necessarily accept a policy of moderation if the price were their own jobs.

As far as the trade unions were concerned, some of these felt that the Labour leadership had 'talked up' the scale of their 1984 victory in order to get the endorsement of the unions. In retrospect, the unions realised that much less had been gained than had been originally claimed. They had been given no time to consider the deal and had been 'bounced' into accepting it by the party leadership. They would be looking at the details of any 1985 settlement much more carefully.

Local discontents

Another possibility was that Labour would once more postpone all the hard financial decisions in 1985 by setting a compromise budget with a moderate rate rise. In effect they could run a deficit budget, and end up hopelessly overspent at the end of the year. The results could then be presented to the electorate in 1986. Ironically, 1985 would have been the year for the four-yearly Merseyside County Council elections, but because this had been abolished by the Government there would be no election in Liverpool in 1985. If they were endorsed in 1986, Labour could go back to the Government and say they had popular support for illegality and ask for money to bail out the city. If Labour was defeated in the 1986 council election, the Liberals and Conservatives would be left in a virtually impossible financial mess.

In fact some party members believed Labour might well have trouble in the 1986 elections anyway. Since its success in May 1984 the party had had a difficult time. Its support then had drawn on a deep well of anti-Thatcherism in Liverpool as much as upon a positive endorsement of its illegal policies. Since then some dissatisfaction had set in and the party had lost by-elections in two marginal wards in the city, one of them extremely badly. Throughout the year a number of issues threatened to challenge the popular unity which had marked the Labour council's campaign against the Conservative Government in 1984.

Some of Labour's problems were inherited from the lost decade of coalition politics. For example, the Labour council had done in less than a year what nobody else had done in a decade, by getting a comprehensive re-organisation plan for the secondary schools sector approved. But the scheme had upset many people. Although the Government accepted the council's plan, it received 70,000 objections. The backwash from that during its implementation hung over the council in 1985.

Labour also got into enormous difficulty over the most prosaic of services, refuse collection. Not only had Patrick Jenkin made people in the city realise it was extremely expensive, but at various times during the year the service seemed to have collapsed, as the bins were not emptied for almost a month and rubbish piled up in the streets. The council's critics argued the problems were caused by union restrictive practices, featherbedding and inefficiency in the workforce. Labour replied that the failure stemmed from previous Liberal administrations' refusal to spend money and invest in stock, which meant the existing wagons were too old, constantly being repaired and unable to cope with the demand. In fact, both arguments were true. But the expense and poor quality of the service damaged the council. After two years in power, Labour realised it could hardly ask people to vote for them and support a campaign to defend local services if they were all as bad as the bin service.

By the spring Labour was confronting the unions on the need to improve the service, pointing to the party's defeat in two by-elections as evidence that the city would not tolerate such poor services. The unions would either have to co-operate with Labour's reforms or run the risk of the party losing control and the Liberals privatising the service. However, it was not easy for the council to avoid union disputes and a strike by a tiny number of maintenance men over bonus schemes paralysed refuse collection in June 1985. Just when the confrontation with the Government over the defence of local services was entering its most serious phase, the public parks were being opened as temporary tips, because the council could not get the bins emptied.

Labour also had difficulties with a group of natural supporters, the council tenants, who had expected the party to tackle the problems of an expensive, demoralised, badly managed and inefficient direct labour organisation which gave tenants a terribly bad repairs and maintenance service. By the spring the council had mounted a major public attack on the organisation, and recruited a highly paid officer from outside the city to deal with the unions and reform management and labour practices. But its initial slowness in tackling the problem again weakened its argument that it was defending local services. These were all difficult managerial problems which Labour had inherited, not created. The administration of the city had become so slack during the coalition era that the Labour council was bound to face awkward, unpopular decisions. However, it was at least addressing them.

Some other problems were of the party's own making. There were constant accusations by the opposition parties about patronage within the Labour administration. There were rumbling conflicts between the council and its white-collar employees over management decisions – the internal reorganisation of departments, the increased use of special administrative units which by-passed existing departments, the growing isolation of chief officers and the alleged political appointment of Militant supporters to local authority jobs. These matters had come to a controversial head in the previous November.

The council had created a new race relations unit in the authority and they appointed as its director a 26-year old black quantity surveyor from London, Samson Bond, who had little experience and few formal qualifications in the field. The appointment, and the way it was subsequently handled, caused an uproar, with many representatives of the black community arguing that Bond was a Militant appointee. NALGO were equally unhappy and boycotted the post. The blacks physically harrassed Bond, and later attacked Labour councillors. At one point the blacks themselves were thrown out of the council chamber by the police. A Labour councillor resigned in protest at the policy. The Bond affair continued into 1985, causing great bitterness, and reinforcing some worries about the responsiveness of the Labour council to community opinion. At the same time there were disputes with the voluntary sector over the council's alleged efforts to weaken or municipalise voluntary projects. The council's municipal housing strategy which had led it to abandon or municipalise a number of housing cooperatives, many of them in working-class areas, caused continuing conflict.

In 1984 Liverpool's voters had shown enormous support for the Labour party's defiance of the Government – its refusal to get rid of council workers, to reduce its services or make local people pay for Government cutbacks. The risk for the council was that the need to sort out its services and its alienation from some groups in the city, would dissipate some of that support. Worries about the secretiveness of party decision-making and the dogmatic character of some of its policies, were beginning to expose political divisions. The Labour leaders replied that a party intent on governing was bound to break a few eggs. It was not clear if everyone would see it that way.

Getting stuck behind rate-capping

But there was another pressure on the council in 1985 which had a far more critical effect on the denouement of the crisis. This time the city was not alone in challenging the Government. In 1984, Liverpool had been accused of irresponsibility for breaking ranks with the national Labour Party. In 1985 Liverpool stayed in line with Labour's orchestrated national protest against rate-capping. The Labour council had gone it alone in 1984 because it did not think the other authorities would be 'hard' enough in the confrontation with the Government. The events of 1985 only confirmed its predictions.

From the start there were important differences of opinion about strategy amongst the Labour authorities. They tended to be dominated by the London boroughs, who had more professional, middle class, inner city parties, without Liverpool's strong links to the manual workers' unions, the district Labour party or the Militant Tendency. They certainly did not have the severity of Liverpool's financial problems. They opted for a policy of refusing to set a rate in 1985/86, until the Government made financial concessions to them.

Liverpool had wanted the group to adopt a 'deficit budget' strategy. For Liverpool, the danger with the 'no rates' strategy was that individual authorities might fall by the wayside and slowly start setting rates once the pressures upon them increased. The campaign could begin to disintegrate and leave the Government facing a very exposed and vulnerable minority who could then be easily picked off by the courts. However, Liverpool agreed to adopt the policy to maintain common unity.

The protesting authorities held together during the phoney war in the autumn of 1984. But in the spring of 1985, when the reality of individual disqualification, surcharge and bankruptcy loomed nearer, and concerns about the Labour Party breaking the law grew, nerves began to fail in many authorities. Ironically, Liverpool's apparent success in 1984 had encouraged the authorities to confront the Government in the first place. But it had also taught the Government how to play the game. After some initial correspondence with the group, Patrick Jenkin simply refused to meet them in the spring. He had not forgotten his lesson from Liverpool in 1984 and it helped him to defeat the larger campaign in 1985.

On 7 March, all the authorities duly refused to set a rate for 1985/86. But under the threat of legal action, and facing Jenkin's refusal to concede ground, the campaign slowly disintegrated, with individual authorities giving in with varying degrees of confusion and recrimination. The metropolitan counties, under a different legal obligation than the district councils to set a rate, went first in an initial wave after 7 March. But the districts soon followed. Some authorities, like Merseyside and Sheffield, tried to keep the struggle going by setting a rate which might eventually lead them to run out of money at the end of the financial year and provoke a confrontation then. However, the collective resistance was defused. The Labour leaders believed that if only four or five councils had held out, the Government would have faced a very different position. But it did not happen.

As Liverpool's councillors feared, the debacle of the rate-capping campaign muddied the waters for Liverpool. It meant that they were not in control of the tactics, but had to support them anyway. They could not dominate the confrontation but had to share a stage with the other authorities, so that their case for special treatment for the city got lost in the welter of other claims. And it had a crucial effect on the timing of their own decision-making.

Enter the district auditor

At the beginning of June the pressures that had been building up on the

Labour council for almost two years finally exploded. In one frenetic week a whole series of events bore down on it. The first was the district auditor's actions. For over a year, the Labour group had ignored the auditor's warnings. Even as he gave his last one on 24 May – that they should make a rate by 1 June – they thought he was bluffing. But they did believe their senior officers. Their last formal legal advice came in April. This argued that every day that the council failed to make a rate after 1 April increased the risk of legal action against them, but it emphasised that 20 June was the crucial date. After that the legal position might become irretrievable, as it would be administratively impossible for the authority to give the ratepayers their legal right to pay their annual rate bill in ten monthly instalments.

The officers believed if that happened, the auditor would have a much stronger legal case against the council. Before that deadline, it would be less obvious. Since the council typically received little rate income in April, May or June, but did receive its Government grant, it was not precisely clear how an auditor could prove that a real loss had occurred at that time amidst all the flows of the city's income and expenditure. As it turned out, the auditor thought differently. However, the Labour leaders called an emergency meeting of the council on 14 June which would allow time to set a legal rate, if that was what they intended to do. This became Labour's deadline.

The timing was complicated by the national campaign against rate-capping. Even though the Labour leaders always believed the other authorities would finally buckle under to the Government, this took a lot longer than they had expected. At the beginning of June 1985 several authorities were still refusing to set a rate. Although most very quickly gave way, in the last days before Liverpool had to make a rate, the London borough of Lambeth was still holding out. They were, in John Hamilton's words, 'the joker in the pack.' If the Labour council had ever intended to blame the soft left nationally for abandoning Liverpool and leaving it isolated, so that it might then present a compromise budget, it could not play that card while another authority was still resisting.

This was especially true since the leader of Lambeth council, Ted Knight, had a Workers' Revolutionary Party background, and might be happy to accuse Militant Liverpool of 'bottling out' of the confrontation. The in-joke at the time was that Liverpool and Lambeth were playing chicken in the road to see who would be the first to move – but they both got run down. However, that was a minor theme. The major one was that Liverpool had always hoped that the national campaign might provoke a response from the Government and that serious talks would be held. But the Government stuck to its guns. By the time it was absolutely clear that the national campaign had failed, the Labour leaders were almost up against their mid-June deadline.

Setting an illegal rate

In fact the key leaders, Byrne, Hatton and Mulhearn, only began to examine their options jointly during the first week in June. They knew they had few real political choices. Tony Byrne was the only one who fully understood the figures and the minimum he could get the 1985/86 expenditure down to was £m252, which would need a 75 per cent rate rise. It could rise to £m270, with a rate rise of 120 per cent needed. These increases were immediately ruled out as politically unacceptable. The leaders then tried to find some compromise rate rise which would not balance the books but might allow the city to get at least close to the end of the financial year before the money ran out, and might be acceptable to the unions and the party. This produced a figure of a 20 per cent rate rise. Finally a notional single figure increase of 9 per cent was selected as a way of setting a clearly illegal rate. This figure had no budgetary significance; it was a symbolic commitment to resistance.

The first meeting of the crucial budget week took place on Monday night, 10 June. This was between the Labour leaders and key senior union officials. Before the meeting, the union leaders believed that the Labour group would move a compromise budget with a 20 per cent rate rise. They were surprised to find this did not happen. Only Tony Byrne made a major speech and he merely rehearsed the alternative figures making no clear recommendation as between 9 and 20 per cent. But he did suggest that a 20 per cent rise might not bring in enough money to last the year. The Labour leaders also asked the unions to bring out their members in a strike which would close down the city in one week's time, as a gesture of support for the council.

Whether or not the Labour leaders expected the unions to recommend a 20 per cent rate rise, they did not do so. Instead, the unions withdrew to discuss the offer privately. Peter Cresswell, of NALGO argued that if it meant that the city would run out of money and the last three months of the year would be spent with unions squabbling over whose members would have to sacrifice their jobs, there was no point going for 20 per cent. If it was going to mean redundancies anyway, the unions might as well fight the Conservative Government and its commissioners, as fight the Labour council. The key blue-collar union leader, Peter Lennard, who represented the politically more militant, low-paid council workers, for whom a large rate rise meant a real pay cut, needed no persuading that the only option was a 9 per cent rise. When they returned to the meeting, the union leaders would not promise the strike and they were non-committal on the rate rise. But they did not recommend 20 per cent. So the unions did not force the Labour leadership to go for broke. They simply refused to get them off the horns of their dilemma. They would not be seen taking the lead and recommending a compromise.

Neither was there grass-roots support for a compromise. As the leaders took soundings in the wards, especially those dominated by the Militants, they got the message back that a compromise was not acceptable. If the Militant leaders wanted a compromise, it quickly became very clear that their rank and file would not buy it. They had been talked into believing the party would not go for a 'massive' rate rise, and they would not allow one.

On top of that, many back bench councillors, non-Militant as well as Militant, argued that the party should not set a big rate rise. For many of them, the only principled position was to confront the issue directly and force the Government's hand. As one backbencher explained – 'I'm not a Marxist, I don't even believe in all this political stuff. I just don't think its fair. And I wouldn't vote for anything but a 9 per cent increase.' Another non-Militant councillor, who had been involved in the election disaster after Labour's 50 per cent rate rise in 1980, had assumed that the leadership would move a 20 per cent rise and had wrestled with his conscience all week about breaking Labour's promise not to impose 'massive' rate rises. Finally he had decided to oppose the 20 per cent and move a lower one; he was intensely relieved to find that 9 per cent was finally chosen.

Another backbencher, a successful solicitor who would be debarred from practising if he were bankrupted, was offered a dispensation from supporting the illegal rate by his ward party. But he refused the offer and eventually voted with the group. Any political differences within the group between the Militants and non-Militants were overwhelmed by their unity on this issue. It would be the worst of all worlds to compromise in 1985, get accused of treachery, and then find they could not manage on the money, and end up in court anyway. Even if they lasted the year, the councillors felt they could not campaign a third time on the argument that the city was in serious financial trouble and still expect the public to believe them. By the end of the week, the Militant and non-Militant leaders realised that if they did try to present a compromise figure, they might even split the Labour group in the council on budget day.

The decision to go for a 9 per cent rate rise was actually made at the Militant-dominated executive committee of the district Labour party on Wednesday night, 12 June. The meeting only lasted fifty minutes and there was no serious discussion of any alternative figure. By that time, nobody was willing to be seen pushing for the compromise figure. As the leading shopsteward for the manual workers, Ian Lowes, pointed out 'nobody, whatever their politics, could have got a 20 per cent rate rise through the district party.' In other words, the national and local Militant leadership could not have controlled their rank and file even if they wanted to do anything else.

The executive committee resolution was considered by a packed district Labour party meeting on Thursday, 13 June. This was now a formality. The district party instructed the councillors not to make a legal rate. There were no alternatives and no opposition from the floor. Nearly all the Labour councillors were present but none dissented. One of the few amendments was made by the secretary of the blue-collar union, which insisted that the councillors should not vote for a compromise budget, even if there were any defections in the group the following day. The resolution was accepted unanimously. By this time the Labour leaders were not engaged in debate. They were rallying the troops.

The Labour group met briefly after the district party meeting and with the adrenalin still flowing, all the hands went up in favour of the illegal budget. As one councillor put it, they 'reacted to the war cry like troops being sent over the top.' The crucial question was whether all the councillors would stick to their guns the next day at the council budget meeting. Until the very last moment on Friday morning, there were doubts that all the backbenchers would vote for illegality. But, like everyone else, they had been overtaken by events, as the leadership's decision to go for 9 per cent only became final on Wednesday night, which gave them just one day to make up their minds. Also, there was an enormous emotional pressure on the group to stand firm and not defect like the 'traitors' in 1984.

But there was one final blow. The district auditor wrote to the councillors at the beginning of the week telling them that, since they had ignored his warnings to make a rate by 1 June, he was not waiting any longer. Their crime had already been committed and he was acting against them for the losses they had incurred between 1 April and June. It did not matter to him what rate, if any, they set on 14 June. The timing could not have been worse. For any councillors thinking of defecting, this was the last straw. They were already in danger of being surcharged, disqualified and bankrupted. There was no point running the gauntlet of defection if they were already outside the law. In John Hamilton's words, the district auditor 'shotgunned' the group into its decision. There could be no retreat. Everyone in the party was now saying 'you might as well be hung for a sheep as a lamb.'

The council considered Labour's budget at 9 o'clock on Friday morning, June 14. In contrast to the wild mood of previous meetings, a sombre atmosphere lay over the chamber. Hardly any information was presented apart from one brief page of figures; there was no explanation of the final budget figure of £m265. Once the deficit of almost £m6 from 1984/85 was added to that base of £m265, the city needed to spend over £m270. At that level, the penalties imposed would cut the rate support grant from £m118 to £m29. The city would then have to find £m242 from the rates. A 9 per cent rate rise would produce only £m125 and the city would be £m117 short of the money it needed for the year. On that scenario it would never make it and was bound to run out of money.

The numbers in the council chamber on 14 June the day meant that if only three more Labour councillors had joined the original Labour defectors and voted with the opposition, the budget would have been defeated. But to the obvious amazement of the opposition parties who had constantly predicted the group's collapse, 49 Labour councillors voted for illegality and bankruptcy, after only just over two hours of debate. As they left the chamber, the consequences of their actions were still sinking in to many of them. John Hamilton looked weary and crestfallen. But others were glad to have done it regardless of the consequences: they were simply relieved to get off the emotional roller-coaster they had been on for two years.

The council's senior officers were shattered by the decision. The Government was equally stunned. For months their intelligence had told them that Liverpool would back down. The civil servants who were sending the memos down to London could scarcely believe their contents. The council's action seemed beyond reason. The following week, the Cabinet committee of senior Ministers led by the Prime Minister, who had monitored the crisis in 1984, met again to decide what to do. They had very few options. As a senior civil servant said 'we can either sit on our hands or dust off the commissioner file from last year. The commissioner option looks as unattractive this year as it did last. It's just too uncertain.'

The one option Ministers did consider was whether they should ask the Attorney General to take the case to the High Court, get the rate quashed and the council instructed to set a new legal rate. That move was open. But it was risky. It would be an olive branch to the Labour council who could then set a legal rate and wipe out their previous illegal act. However, the Government was worried that the council would only exploit the covert offer and argue that it had forced the Government to back down again. Even more alarming, if the High Court set aside the first rate, and the Labour council simply refused to set any rate at all, the city would be without income almost immediately and might collapse very quickly indeed. The Government was frightened of bringing the pack of cards down on its head. All the advice it was getting from Liverpool was that the Labour group was completely locked into its position with absolutely no prospect that it would behave 'responsibly' if the Government gave it a second bite at the cherry. Ministers sat around the table gradually realising the position that their policies on local Government finance had finally led them to. They were drifting towards the confrontation they never really wanted with no apparent way of avoiding it.

The Ministers decided to sit on their hands, hoping that something would turn up. But they had no idea what this might be. As one civil servant put it 'the Government only really has one big weapon to use – the commissioners. When they've used it, they've used it.' It was unlikely that anyone else would quash the rate. The Liverpool Chamber of Commerce thought about it, but decided against it. The leaders of the opposition parties considered it but, quite apart from the expense involved in legal action, there were political imperatives not to do so. They might be accused of bringing the house down. More important, they would have to suggest a higher rate to be set and, given the mood in the city, that could only damage them with the electorate. Everybody was waiting and wondering about the next move.

The Labour group's reaction was to start up its publicity campaign again, focusing on the threats of non-elected officials getting rid of the people's elected representatives. Its real target was the workforce and the unions. Even at the last, Derek Hatton believed that a massive demonstration of support by the workforce would persuade the Government to give Liverpool the money it was asking for. He believed Thatcher had made concessions to Liverpool in 1984 because of the pressure Liverpool had exerted upon her. Liverpool would have to do that again.

The Labour leaders directed their campaign at the workforce at dozens of meetings, asking them to 'lock up' the city if the Government made a move against them. But because of the almost complete political and financial confusion, the workforce was not sure how to react to Labour's illegality. The joint shop stewards committee voted in favour of industrial action if legal action was taken against the councillors. As its chairman, Peter Cresswell, put it, the unions were neither the paymasters nor the innocent dupes of the Labour party. They were not defending heroic gestures. They simply believed that the council faced either huge cuts in jobs or very large rate rises, and the unions were opposed to both. They had to support the council, whatever reservations they had. But nobody was quite sure what that meant, nor when the action would take place – whether it would be if the councillors got a note of disqualification from the district auditor or whether it would be after the councillors were finally disqualified after appeal, which would take months.

Some blue-collar workers, who possibly had most to lose if Labour lost office, were willing to 'have a go' as soon as they were asked. It was well known that the security force and the caretakers were willing to lock the commissioners out of the authority's buildings. The white-collar workers were more ambivalent. The teachers actually voted against a very moderate proposal to defend their own jobs – not the councillors – with industrial action. But even if the unions were to take industrial action and hold a day or even a one-week strike as canvassed, it was not clear to many how this could change the Government's position anyway. In fact, the Government now believed that the matter was out of its hands. It was not willing to make financial concessions to Liverpool. In the Government's view, the matter was now in the hands of the law, the district auditor and the financial markets.

'Wilful misconduct'

The months from June through September were full of confusion, suspicion and rumour. Would the Government pay the rate support grant to Liverpool; would the banks lend money; if not when would the city run out of money; would anyone take the council to court; would the Government send its commissioners; what would the district auditor do; would the services collapse; would the council workers lose their jobs? Nobody seemed to know what would happen. There was little mutual trust around, and less accurate information, either about what was happening or about other people's motives and intentions. This got much worse after 14 June. Nobody, for example, was clear whether the Labour council had really meant to do what it had done, or whether it had stumbled into the position and wanted to get out of it. And hardly anyone except Tony Byrne and the treasurer, Michael Reddington, knew whether there was any chance of rescuing the situation anyway. However, some things soon became clear.

The first was that national elites would not budge. Derek Hatton spoke to the Labour Party's national executive committee seeking support. That produced a carefully worded motion defending Labour councils, attacking the Government and asking for the district auditor to be called off. However, Neil Kinnock was on television ten minutes after it was released saying this did not mean they supported illegality. Patrick Jenkin refused to meet the council. Liverpool's MPs managed after some effort to get a meeting with Jenkin, but no concessions. Jenkin suggested that the council take its own case to the High Court, get the illegal rate quashed, and start again with a new rate. John Cunningham wrote to Patrick Jenkin suggesting talks, at the request of the council. But he knew beforehand that Jenkin would turn him down. Which he did.

The next move was made by Tim McMahon, the district auditor. On 26 June, McMahon started proceedings against 49 Labour councillors whom he thought were guilty of incurring 'losses' by 'wilful misconduct.' In his view, the council had already lost money by not collecting its rates on time and having to pay interest charges on the money it had borrowed to cover for them. Since the city treasurer had calculated that the delay in setting a rate might have cost the city £m1.2 in interest charges in 1984, McMahon indicated the councillors might end up being charged with that kind of money. But as the figures would not be entirely clear until the end of the financial year, he was not proceeding with that for the time being.

Instead he argued he could immediately assess a different loss. This arose in the following way. The Government had paid the first instalment of the city's rate support grant, on the assumption that it would actually spend at its target level. The payment would be adjusted once the Government got detailed information about the city's budget in July. That was customary. But by failing to make a rate on time the city had not received two other payments from the Government. The Department of Health and Social Security, which subsidises the housing benefits scheme that the local authority directly administers, had not paid the council the first three monthly instalments worth £m6. And the Treasury had not paid the first of two bi-annual instalments it normally paid the council instead of rates on Crown property. Since Jenkin had announced in Parliament in March that no authority would receive either of those grants until they set a rate, McMahon argued the council had incurred the loss by its wilful misconduct. He calculated that the council had lost potential interest of almost £3,000 a day from not having that money to invest. By 24 June these losses amounted to over £106,000. As that was now over £2,000 for each councillor involved they were liable for disqualification from office as well as surcharging. He gave the councillors three weeks to explain why they should not be disqualified.

The council replied on 19 July. In a thirty-page document, they argued that there was no legal date by which an authority had to set a rate. The judge in the most recent court case had set a limit of 1 June, but had said each case had to be individually considered. It pointed out that in 1984 the district auditor had told Liverpool that 20 June, not 1 June, was the crucial date for setting a rate. The council's senior officers had emphasised the importance of this date. And the council had in fact set a rate before that date. The councillors had never individually or collectively said they would not set a rate for 1985/86. Far from neglecting the financial interests of the ratepayers, the council argued it had made every effort to increase its resources to deal with the city's 'distressing social conditions', rehearsing all the negotiations it had had with the Government on its housing and urban programme. It argued that its budget was delayed because the Government had delayed decisions on important bids for urban programme money, which dramatically affected the council's spending plans.

The council also repeated its objections to the grant system made in the 'joint report', arguing that since it had had 'a marked measure of success' in getting special help from the Government in 1984/85 after 'spirited negotiations', there was 'every reason' to suppose it would do so again in 1985, especially since other authorities were resisting the Government at the time. On the specific losses, the council argued that, since the Government did not withhold or threaten to withhold payment of housing benefit subsidy in 1984 even though Liverpool had set its rate later than in 1985, it was fully entitled and expected to get the same treatment in 1985. The fact that it had not done so was not its fault, but a result of 'the will or whim' of the Government. As Treasury payments on Crown property were essentially the equivalent of rates, that delay had to be seen in the larger context of its justification for delaying setting a rate in the first place. Anyway, in 1984 Liverpool had not got its first payment from the Treasury until 25 July, whereas in 1985 it had got it three weeks earlier on 4 July.

The council's defence, which was nearly all concerned with the detailed politics of the relationship between the Government and the city council during its two years of office, did not turn on whether the losses had been incurred, but whether they were the result of wilful misconduct on its part. Essentially the Labour council argued that it intended to offset any short-term losses with extra Government money. The district auditor had accepted this in 1984. He should do so again in 1985. That was what McMahon would have to make up his mind about by September 1985. Publicly, the leaders had been confident they would win the case. Privately, many back-benchers admitted to being terrified.

Capital receipts and redundancy notices

But however tragic it might be for individual councillors and their families, by the end of August 1985, the district auditor's case was something of a sideshow, unless the city could make sense of its budget. Liverpool might have collapsed long before the councillors' fate was determined. And this was what was preoccupying the treasurer. Like many of the other senior officers, Michael Reddington was in despair after the 9 per cent rate rise. It prompted desperate efforts on his part to try to get a grip on the position. In early July, the power to authorise any new spending was taken away from chief officers and given to Tony Byrne as chairman of the finance and strategy committee in order to limit spending as well as to transfer legal liability from officers to politicians. A 'star' chamber was set up to examine all requests for new spending. This started a rapid examination of all the financial options open to the council to reduce spending in 1985/86. By the end of the month, these efforts had paid a dividend. The base budget had been cut by £m10 down to £m255, mainly by creative accounting.

Reddington pointed out that many of these manoeuvres stored up longer term financial problems and were undesirable. But this no longer mattered in view of the crisis facing the city. Reddington had calculated in early July that the 9 per cent rate rise would only produce £m229 in income and that the city was already contractually committed to spending £m171 in the year, including the three months' redundancy pay its employees would have to be paid. The city had to spend a further £m5 a week beyond that to keep going. By late July, the Government had told Reddington that Liverpool should get £m29 grant in 1985/86. But it had already received over £m37 in the first instalment, so it would be getting no more. In late July the Public Works Loan Board told Reddington he could borrow no more from them until Liverpool set a legal rate and budget. He had to borrow in the private market and pay a gradually increasing premium in interest rates for doing so.

Reddington soon would not be able to borrow any more money to keep his revenue budget going, because he would not be able to guarantee he could repay the loans. Quite apart from questions of professional propriety, he might be liable to criminal charges if he continued to borrow in those circumstances. The local authority treasurers' professional association had already become so concerned about the position that in mid-July it had taken legal advice about how their members should behave when managing deficit budgets. This only reinforced Reddington's view about the short time he had left in which he could continue to borrow to keep the city afloat.

On 19 July, McMahon wrote to the councillors again, warning them he might take further action against them for their 9 per cent rate rise. But his immediate purpose was to tell the council what he thought Reddington's deadline was – the end of September. He gave the council three choices: find ways of cutting its services or spending; go to the High Court, get the original rate quashed and set a new one that would pay the bills; or start preparing redundancy notices for its 30,000 employees.

There was one other option open to the council. The treasurer's report of 31 July had shown that in the revenue budgets for the two years 1984/85 and 1985/86, there was up to £m27 of work in housing repairs and maintenance which might be called capital work. Because this was not new building, as long as it was paid from existing capital receipts and not from borrowing, it would avoid the limit the Government placed on the city's capital spending. If enough capital receipts could be found, they could reduce the revenue budget by £m27.

However, all the capital receipts the city was allowed to spend were needed for its massive house-building programme, which was running at £m112 in 1985/86. But as part of a policy to increase the money available to pay for the programme in future, Reddington had negotiated a deferred payment deal with a stockbroking firm, Philips and Drew, in which it would pay £m30 to builders for the work done on the housing programme in 1985/86. The city would repay the stockbrokers in later years. Although this money was needed for future years, in principle it could be partly used to reduce the revenue budget from £m255. This would mean the Government grant would then begin to flow back, and the city might get near the end of the financial year before the money ran out. In this way the immediate crisis would be averted.

The problem for the Labour council if it accepted this 'capitalisation' option would be the long-term costs. The city would have to pay interest charges on the loans, which in eight years might actually be as large as the money originally borrowed. More important, the deal would limit the size of the building programme in future years in two ways. The loan would have to be paid back at about £m8 a year, which would have to be deducted from the money that could otherwise be used to pay for house-building for several years to come. Most crucial, if the city used the capital receipts to pay for revenue in 1985/86, the building programme would have to be smaller the following year. In other words, capitalisation would put off the revenue crisis to 1986. But it would limit the council house building and the jobs it created.

If the city had many more capital receipts in the bank it would be different. But it would already be using in various ways the £m60 capital receipts which had been accumulated in the past few years to finance both the city's revenue and capital programme in 1985/86. It could not easily generate that amount of money again. There is not that much to sell. And the money could only be spent once. It would only postpone the revenue problem until the following year, when the council would not have the £m20 capital receipts to pay for its jobs and services. They would then either have to be cut or paid for by very large rate increases. The beginning of the new financial year and the prospect of those tough financial decisions was by now only six months away.

However, the Labour leadership insisted that it would not use its housing reserves in this way to balance the revenue budget. The political costs of backing down, and the cost to the housing programme in future, in its view were too great. Tony Byrne argued that the money was needed to pay the wages of the private sector workers who were building council houses for the working classes, not to pay public sector salaries for just another few months. The Labour leaders argued that their whole strategy was to protect jobs in all parts of the city. They would not make the building workers pay the price of keeping local authority workers in jobs. They regarded that as treachery and portrayed anyone who recommended 'capitalisation' as traitors to the party. By contrast, some white-collar leaders believed that capitalisation was the council's 'least bad' option. Labour had wilfully exaggerated its costs and rejected it in favour of confrontation with the Conservative Government.

So the Labour leadership developed a new plan. It dropped its demand for the return of the £m30 the Government had 'stolen'. It realised that this was not going to work. Instead, it asked the Government to let the council borrow an extra £m25, which would allow it to balance the books and keep the city running. Labour argued that if this did not happen, the city would collapse and the Government would be responsible. But it also made contingency plans if the Government would not allow the borrowing. The council would keep enough money to pay for absolutely minimal emergency services only – providing residential care for the elderly, sheltering the homeless, doing emergency repairs, protecting public health, burying the dead. All other services would eventually have to cease. Because there would be no money left to pay them, the council would begin moves to terminate the contracts of all employees. The council's officers had advised the Labour leaders that they had to do this under the 1978 Employment Protection Act. If they did not do so, the employees would be able to sue the council for salaries, even if there was no money left. And it was quite possible that the individual councillors would eventually be held personally responsible for the millions of pounds involved. They intended to reinstate the workers as soon as possible, and certainly when the new financial year began in April 1986 and the local authority would be back in business again.

This all came as a great shock to the Labour leadership, who had never thought about these kinds of legal implications. It came as an even greater shock to the unions. The political consequences of that move blew Labour's campaign wide open. When the plan was revealed during the first week in September 1985 it caused an uproar which locked the unions and the Labour council into a furious and damaging argument. Union leaders simply refused to accept redundancy. They argued that they had always known that the money would one day run out and they would not be paid. But in two years of crisis, there had never been any mention of redundancies, which would jeopardise their jobs, and eliminate all their legal protection provided under the Act. They would have no guarantee that they would get their jobs back once the city started running again. Even if they did get them back, the interruption of service would mean that for a further two years they would not regain the legal protection of the Act. Throughout the first week of September, confusion reigned as the Labour leaders frantically tried to find a form of words which would satisfy the unions that they would not in fact lose their jobs. Derek Hatton went back and forth between meetings with the unions and council's senior officers. But it was impossible. No amount of massaging the fine print could alter the basic legal position.

On Thursday, 6 September 1985, the council finally announced its contingency plans – employees' existing contracts would 'cease to exist' on 18 December. Finally, the implications of the alliance between the unions and the Labour council became clear. Whereas for almost two years the unions had identified their interests with those of the council in its fight against the Government, they now began to recognise the division of interest between the council as employer and themselves as employees.

At the same time, the redundancy threat revealed the difference of interest between blue-collar and white-collar unions that had been broadly concealed for two years. The division broke out into the open on Friday, 7 September, when after meetings between the council leaders and the leaders of the 'General and Municipal' that union did a complete volte face and decided to support the redundancy plan. The explanation was simple. When the lower paid blue-collar workers received their redundancy payment and unemployment benefit, they would be financially better off than if they were working. Since the Government would have to pay one-third of the total redundancy bill, as well as the unemployment benefit, the council could score a propaganda victory by arguing that the Government had paid more to make the employees redundant than if they had given Liverpool its £m30 in the first place. Also if redundancy notices were issued, the city would in effect be solvent until the end of the financial year. The Labour council would then have until December to run its campaign against the Government.

But the plan disintegrated at a meeting of the Joint Shop Stewards on Saturday, 7 September, in a long and bitter debate between blue-collar and white-collar unions. Whereas the blue-collar workers were confident of being reinstated by the Labour council, the white-collar workers feared that many of them would not be, and they would have no legal redress. Amidst much recrimination, the plan to accept redundancy was narrowly beaten by 51 votes to 48. Amidst the chaos, one blue-collar worker shouted that the unions would have to surround the Town Hall the following Monday, lock the Labour councillors out of the building and prevent their issuing redundancy notices. And this indeed happened. This move dramatically escalated the financial crisis. Instead of running out of money in December as Labour planned, the city would be immediately unable to borrow in the market and it could be bankrupt in less than three weeks.

Breaking ranks

Immediately after this lock-out the shop stewards' committee met to consider the next move in another angry and bitter meeting. Despite the opposition of NALGO, the blue-collar workers vetoed the capitalisation plan and proposed instead an indefinite strike to force the Government to give the city £m30. But the white-collar leaders would not even consider a strike until they had a guarantee of no redundancy. They argued they could not get their members out on an indefinite strike. Nor could they understand where it would lead.

Finally the vote was taken and the strike call won by 56 votes to 44. At this point tempers were running very high indeed. The blue-collar workers insisted the white-collar workers' leaders should commit themselves to the strike, and called for the doors of the building to be locked until the white-collar leaders agreed. After further acrimonious and abusive debate, the meeting unanimously agreed to put the motion to their members for a strike on 24 September. Derek Hatton then gave NALGO their written undertaking there would be no redundancies.

However, there were doubts from the start whether the white-collar workers would support the strike. By this time the national leaders of the white-collar unions had entered the fray and were trying to postpone the strike call. They were not even clear the strike was legal, since it was a political rather than an industrial strike. In their view the local unions could strike against the council as employer if the money ran out, but not against the Government. The results were announced on the evening of 24 September. The strike call was defeated.

Several union leaders did not even present the strike to their members. Only three unions voted for the strike. But most crucially, the key unions were divided. The 'General and Municipal' was in favour – 4,345 to 2,934. NALGO was opposed – 3,891 to 1,445. After this setback, the Joint Shop Stewards' Executive Committee voted to postpone the indefinite strike but to call for a one-day strike the following day. The strike call had been a tactical disaster for the Labour council. Instead of uniting the unions with the council in a common fight against the Government, it set the unions against each other as well as against the Labour council. Labour had got itself trapped between its friends and its enemies. The failure of the strike call guaranteed that the political recriminations would continue in Liverpool. But it could not change the basic financial position. If there had been a total strike for six weeks and the city did not have to pay its employees, enough money could have been saved to allow the city to last the financial year. Since that had not happened, the council was left facing its original options. It could increase the rate. It would use its housing reserves to capitalise revenue spending and postpone the crisis. Or it could return to the redundancy option.

On 25 September the Labour leaders chose the redundancy option. This would buy them time and allow them to borrow. But the decision guaranteed the continuation of their struggle with the white-collar unions, over capitalisation. On 26 September the Joint Shop Stewards' Committee finally split wide open as the blue-collar leaders endorsed the redundancy plan, and NALGO's representatives walked out of the meeting in protest.

The war of nerves between the Government and the Labour council began again. While national union and the Labour party leaders began to panic at the way in which local troops had got out of hand, the Government – with Kenneth Baker now replacing Patrick Jenkin – was taking an even tougher line. At a meeting with Liverpool MPs on 26 September Baker rejected a request for further borrowing. In his view, the council had not exhausted all possible options. They should either set a new rate or postpone the crisis by 'capitalisation'. And there was now another reason for the Government's hard line. Because Liverpool would be rate capped for the first time in 1986/87 at a spending limit of £m245, in real terms the city would have to be run on about £m30 less than in 1985/86 anyway. The city would have difficulties enough in balancing the books in 1986/87, without the additional burden of paying back borrowed money. That problem lay only six months away and it virtually removed any incentive for the Labour councillors to behave 'sensibly'.

Another disincentive to compromise was that the district auditor had in the meantime rejected the Labour council's appeal against his decision to disqualify or surcharge them. He argued that the delay in setting the rate was a deliberate attempt to blackmail the Government into giving the council extra money and as a recent court case had made clear, that was not 'a good reason to justify a clear breach of duty.' He gave them until the middle of October 1985 to appeal to the High Court. The councillors were nearer to being condemned men. Anway, whatever the legal outcome it would be too late to affect the frantic discussions taking place in September 1985.

Despite the opposition of the white-collar unions on 27 September, the Labour party forced the redundancy motion through the city council. This meant the campaign would continue. Liverpool could find itself without any services between January and April, 1986. In which case, the city would grind to a halt. The workers would not be paid and they would have lost their jobs with no guarantee of getting them back. Only emergency services would be provided. In any event, the dispute between blue- and white-collar workers was bound to get worse as the politics of intimidation set in. And the threat of thirty thousand council workers' jobs would be once more used to encourage the national Labour Party conference to help blackmail the Government into giving the Labour council and Tony Byrne what they desperately wanted – the money for more public housing.

But the Party conference at the beginning of October did not go to plan for Liverpool. Neil Kinnock chose the issue of Militant in Liverpool as a way of stamping his authority on the Labour Party and presenting himself to the electorate as a responsible future Prime Minister. He launched a ferocious attack on the irresponsibility of the Militant tactic which had ended up in 'the grotesque chaos of a Labour council hiring taxis to scuttle round the city handing out redundancy notices to its own workers.' A delegate from the Liverpool branch of the National Union of Public Employees brandished her redundancy notice along with the letter from Derek Hatton guaranteeing the council would make no redundancies.

Derek Hatton had hoped to get support for his own resolution calling for industrial action in support of Liverpool. But in the face of the opposition of the union bosses he did a deal with the NEC spokesman and leader of Sheffield city council, David Blunkett. He withdrew

Liverpool's motion in return for a promise that national Party and union leaders would come to Liverpool to examine the financial position and help them find a solution to the crisis.

Blunkett's move saved Liverpool's face at the conference, but effectively placed the national leaders in the position of having to come up with a plan for Liverpool. Whether they realised it or not, the Labour leadership had repeated the Government's mistake of 1984, by getting sucked into Liverpool's financial affairs. It was running the risk of being scapegoated for the failure to find a painless solution in the same way Patrick Jenkin had been exposed in 1984.

Back in Liverpool, the future remained as uncertain as it always had been in the city's apparently never-ending financial odyssey.

8 CONCLUSION

This book has been about political reactions to Liverpool's economic decline, which has been both chronic and dramatic. That decline has been apparent for over fifty years, but has speeded up enormously in the past decade. In many respects, the process has emphasised the great natural strengths of local people and their communities, some of whom are coping impressively with great adversity while facing very bleak futures. However, it has created in others a sense of despair and alienation from the economic and political mainstream. The belief that national elites do not care very much about Liverpool, has produced a degree of cynicism in the city's public life. And it has encouraged, not only in the Liverpool Labour party, what may be called the politics of frustration.

The behaviour of the Labour council can only be understood in this context. Its reaction to its problems was simply 'to have a go' at the Conservative Government. But this primitive line struck a chord with many people in the city, however much it may also have worried them. The brute facts of economic life in Liverpool made it fertile ground for such thinking, just as it made it fertile ground for the revolutionary Militant Tendency. The Militant developed Liverpool's budget strategy and used it for its larger political purposes; but it could not have just imposed it upon the city in May 1984. The voters realised the Labour council had not invented the city's financial and economic problems, even if it had done its utmost to exploit them. In many eyes, the Government forced the council into its resistance, turning people like John Hamilton, the old-fashioned Quaker school teacher and long-standing Labour leader, into lawbreakers.

The Government's contribution

The Conservative Government made its contribution to Liverpool's crisis with a new grant system in 1981. The city argued that the system asked it to achieve more financially than was reasonable. It had a case. The system is very unsympathetic to Liverpool's dilemma. The target system was designed to punish Labour-controlled authorities who had spent expansively during the 1970s, by cutting their spending in the 1980s. Liverpool was not a big spender then and actually spent less than many other cities. But its targets still required it to cut back in the 1980s as if it had been profligate in the 1970s. By July 1985, the Government had given way to the collective pressure of local authorities and abandoned the target system. Since Liverpool had suffered more than any other city through the sytem, the Government's admission of failure makes the city's claim about the unfairness of its treatment persuasive. In 1984, even the Government's own Audit Commission delivered a withering attack on the unpredictability and irrationality of the system which wholly reinforced Liverpool's arguments.

Liverpool also had a good case about the absence in the grant system of sufficient indicators of economic deprivation such as levels of income, poverty or unemployment. During the past decade, governments of both political parties have defined economic decline as the central issue for urban policy. But the block grant system, which is a local authority's primary source of direct government money, does not build economic deprivation into its calculations of local need in any significant way. If this were made as central to the calculation of a city's grant as it is to the Government's definition of the urban crisis, Liverpool would get more money and its financial difficulties would be more manageable.

Equally, the city had a powerful argument that the scale of its population loss – from 850,000 to 490,000 in thirty years and still continuing at the rate of 10,000 a year – made it virtually impossible to cut expenditure as quickly as its grant fell. Despite all the sophistication of the grant related expenditure assessments, the size of the city's population remains by far the most important determinant of how much grant it gets, almost drowning more subtle indicators of need. Many of those directly involved in the Liverpool saga argued that, even if the city did have to cut its expenditure, the Government's timetable was unreasonable. The Labour leader, John Hamilton, put it most vividly. The Government was asking the Labour council to close institutions, reorganise services, and break union practices in very short order. But, in his words, 'when they tried to close five pits, they had a miners' strike on their hands for almost a year.'

The most constructive view came from one official in the Audit Commission, who suggested that Liverpool should not be given a set of punitive annual targets which became increasingly difficult to achieve. That only increased Labour politicians' resentment and unwillingness to cooperate. Instead, it needed a five year expenditure programme – the equivalent of an International Monetary Fund loan – which would provide the city with a set of realistic policies and financial goals. Liverpool would know what it would have to do to achieve them. In return, the Government would offer a longer term strategy for the city with an agreed revenue and capital budget.

This would eliminate much of the uncertainty surrounding the city's financial position. Even if it did not provide the sums of money that many argue are necessary, it would at least provide a more stable context in which the city's difficult political decisions could be faced. Whether such an agreement around specific figures could be reached, given the practical problems and the ideological views of the current protagonists, is obviously an open question. However, if Liverpool is to put its financial house in order, that kind of timetable would be sensible. No doubt the Government would discover this for itself if it ever did have to run the city with its own commissioners.

The Liberal legacy

Both Liberal and Conservative parties in Liverpool made their contribution to the crisis as well. During the lost decade of coalition politics, the Liberals especially failed to respond adequately to the city's long-term decline and held down council spending and rate rises in a search for popularity and votes. Their endless creative accounting and consistent refusal to increase the rates to cover the real cost of the city's commitments, left serious financial difficulties for the Labour council. In particular, the final Liberal budget which Labour inherited significantly underestimated the real costs of running the city. The Liberal reign also encouraged the crisis in a less obvious way. Its 'natural wastage' policies and threats of privatisation alienated the council workforce and their unions, making them extremely defensive in their protection of the remaining council jobs. This made it more difficult for Labour to contemplate reducing the workforce to balance the books, even if it had wanted to.

In fact, Labour had not expected to win control of the council in May 1983 and was astonished to find itself in office. Some of the election promises it made at the time, like cutting council rents by £2 a week and creating a thousand new council jobs, which caused them enormous financial difficulties when they had to run the city, were as much a propaganda attack on the Liberals as serious policy commitments which they had costed and expected to carry out. It meant that the Labour party came to power with rather more ideological baggage than it might have wanted but from which it was difficult to retreat. Even at the end of its second year of office, Labour was still fighting with the ghost of the Liberal leader, Sir Trevor Jones. The final council debates on bankruptcy were dominated more by Labour's attacks on him than by the fate that awaited the city. The exaggerated rhetoric and intellectual poverty of the political debate during the Liberals' lost decade, also encouraged Labour to make its last stand.

The ideological divide

Many forces pushed the Labour council towards its confrontation with central government. The voters, their professional officers, the unions, the Church leaders could all see that there was a genuine grievance; none of the possible legal solutions would have been popular. The fact remains that the Labour council actually chose to precipitate the crisis by refusing to take the decisions necessary to get the city's finances in order. Their financial problems were not insuperable. A three-year austerity programme would have done it. However, the city would have paid a social and economic price. Also Labour thought it would pay a political price; the voters would reject the party as they did in 1980 for a 50 per cent rate rise. For Labour, under these circumstances, bankruptcy was preferable to treachery.

The source of the conflict was the clash between two ideological responses to urban decline – one municipal socialist, the other free market conservative. By the 1980s, Liverpool's Labour party was committed to municipalisation as a way of protecting people in the city from economic decline and continuing attacks on the public sector by the Conservative Government. Labour defined the proper role of a local authority quite differently from the Government, who insisted that a local authority's job was to provide legally required services as efficiently as possible – not to worry about jobs. The Government would look after that by getting the broader economic framework right. If the two sides would agree on that division of responsibility, the problem would go away. But the Labour council would not agree; the Government had not got the broader economic framework right in Liverpool – it had got it all wrong.

For the Labour party, the council was a crucial employer for 15 per cent of the city's workforce. All its policies were designed to protect and create jobs. Like the level of rate rises and its housing programmes, these manpower policies had assumed intense symbolic significance for Labour. Tony Byrne once argued 'Local authority jobs do not belong to the people who have got them now. They belong to the 60,000 people on the dole and to the six year old children in Liverpool. They are their only hope of ever getting a job in their lives.' But for Patrick Jenkin, this was a completely illegitimate view of a local authority as a form of 'outdoor relief.' There lay the ideological divide. The costs of these policies contributed significantly to the city's financial crisis. However, the Labour council argued it was better for it to pay to keep people in work than for the Government to pay more for them to be on the dole.

The Government was much more concerned about the quality of Liverpool's services. In its view, if the city could manage itself properly, services would improve, costs would decline and the financial difficulties would go away. In his attacks on the Labour council, Patrick Jenkin constantly emphasised that Liverpool had financial difficulties because its refuse collection was too expensive. This trivialised the problem. It was certainly true. But even if that was sorted out, it would have only a marginal impact upon the city's budget. The rate at which savings could be made through increased efficiency in council services would not match the rate at which the city lost money for being deemed an overspender. In fact, the improvements which are necessary in many of the city's services may increase its spending and worsen its financial difficulties.

Labour's tactics

The question remains whether the Labour council adopted the right tactics. Its plan was to blackmail the Government into giving extra money by threatening financial suicide, secure in the belief that the

Government would not take the political risk of letting the city collapse. The strategy worked so well in the first year that, in July 1984, the Labour council held an enormous advantage over the Conservative Government. It had won the battle for both hearts and minds in the city with its council election victory. And with the city's professionals' victory in the 'joint report', the Government had tacitly conceded Liverpool had a case. More important, it had been given extra money for 1984 and promised more help in the future. Though these promises were never made explicit or quantified, there is certainly evidence that the Government was willing to help Liverpool with more money for its housing and urban programmes.

The money in itself would not have solved everything. It would not have eliminated the need to make tough financial choices. Also, there would have been strings attached. Liverpool would have had to make some political concessions to allow Patrick Jenkin to sell the deal in the Cabinet and on the Conservative backbenches. In particular, the Labour council would have had to dilute, at least symbolically, its municipalisation strategy, especially on the housing front. But in return, the council could have continued to negotiate directly with the Government about the city's financial difficulties and could have exploited privately the political advantage it had won. The opportunity for positive engagement was there.

However, some of the Labour leaders did not see the issue in those terms. They lost the opportunity when they publicly exploited their budget 'victory.' They permanently changed the Conservative Government's view of the Liverpool council. By November 1984, the Government was stony faced : the olive branch had been spurned and no more help would be available. When the city's MPs tried to get Patrick Jenkin to talk to the council leaders in July 1985, he simply replied 'They danced on my political grave last year. I do not intend to give them a second opportunity.' As one Labour backbencher put it, 'If a Conservative authority had done that to a Labour Government, I would want to know why they were going to help it a second time.'

In Derek Hatton's view, however, the Conservative Government gave in to political pressure, not to negotiations, in 1984. It would give in to Liverpool with more money again in 1985 because it was frightened of having to run the city. But at the same time a senior civil servant in

London categorically denied any money would be given. 'We would come to Liverpool with great reluctance and much injured innocence' he said. 'But we would come.' This Militant tactic – the making of impossible demands – not only alienated the Conservative Government and some people locally, it also angered the national Labour Party leadership as well. In view of Liverpool's long-term dependence upon government money, whichever party is in power, it seemed to many a very high-risk strategy indeed.

Liverpool's future – private sector solutions?

Social justice and self-interest – the 1981 Toxteth riots are still fresh in the Government's memory – mean that public money will continue to come to Liverpool. The question is, how much and how should it best be used? The city does get money from a wide variety of Government Departments, agencies and programmes, but the detailed work necessary to draw up a reliable balance sheet of gains and losses in recent years has not been carried out. However, we do know that for many years the city benefited less than others from regional policy as this provided grant aid for the manufacturing sector – but not the service sector which dominates Liverpool's economy. Similarly, the Government's focus on job creation through small businesses is less likely to be successful in a city like Liverpool which has been dominated by large employers and has little tradition of small firms, as opposed, for example, to its neighbour Manchester which is a regional capital with a large indigenous small-firm sector.

More important, a great deal of Government expenditure in the city does not pay for long-term productive investment as much as it does for the costs of increased unemployment. Some estimates are that as much as 10 per cent of all Government spending in the city goes on the dole. The cost of all unemployment-related benefits has been calculated at £m400 a year, which is considerably more than the Government gives to the city council, the county council and Merseyside Development Corporation put together. The Liverpool Labour party has constantly argued that public money would be better used to protect jobs and improve the public infrastructure by building decent housing for people, even if they had no work. Whatever the flaws in their detailed policies, the Government still has to reply to that case.

Conservative Government policy is to achieve economic recovery by rolling back the boundaries of the state, cutting public expenditure and taxation, and encouraging the private sector and the market to bring growth. The evidence is that such a policy has not, and will not work, in Liverpool. The private sector has abandoned the city at an alarming rate in recent years, despite the fact that its rate levels were relatively low. The public sector did not crowd the private sector out of Liverpool. It left of its own accord. In the past six years, the number of manufacturing jobs in the city has been halved. The only growth to take place during the past decade has been in the public sector.

Moreover, where the private sector has played a visible part in economic redevelopment – in tourism and leisure projects, the creation of a technology park, the recovery of derelict public housing for sale – they have actually been public sector-led projects. The investment of substantial Government money has taken the risk out, or guaranteed the profit, for private investment. Though the best are successful in their own terms, at the moment they are like oases in the desert. If confidence in the city's economy is to be restored, the public sector will have to play a major role.

Similarly, current Government policy is to privatise public housing. This reduces the quality of the remaining public housing stock and the money available for its improvement. This would be more sensible if the demand for private housing and people's capacity to pay for it were clearer. As it is, the proportion of people in public housing is higher in Liverpool than the national average, and estimates are that demand for private housing in the city is 10 per cent lower than the national figure. Low income, lack of job security and high rates of unemployment have forced many potential purchasers out of the private housing market.

Also, if the goal of national policy is to encourage the private market to concentrate resources in those areas which are already economically buoyant and to make other areas wait until enough growth has taken place to fund regeneration, then Liverpool's economy will deteriorate during the next decade. Moreover, even if the private sector does work for some people, the benefits will be unequally shared. The private sector will not redistribute opportunity and rewards towards the underprivileged. There will be increasing inequality and social polarisation with the very poorest in an economic ghetto. Already, there are two parallel labour markets – the core employed and the marginal and unemployed. The gap between the two will inevitably widen, as the level of public provision on which the unemployed depend, continues to fall. As there is 'comfortable' and 'uncomfortable' Britain, so there will be, increasingly, 'comfortable' and 'uncomfortable' Liverpool. After the riots in the Autumn of 1985, the social consequences hardly need underlining.

Wealth creation and welfare are not mutually exclusive. They both have to be the goal of urban policy, tailored to the needs of individual cities. The Government might argue that the only fair way of allocating resources is according to nationally agreed formulae and with this system one cannot treat each city differently. However, it already does so in many ways. For example, the urban programme accepts that cities can spend some of their money in different ways, according to their individual needs. The actual process of allocating the urban programme money to different cities is not done strictly on the basis of any formulae, but rather through Ministerial discretion. It is often argued that Glasgow has enjoyed some economic growth in recent years because of the operation of the very powerful Scottish Development Agency, which has enough resources and powers to guide economic development to it. Liverpool itself has had a battery of special agencies and programmes, even though they have not had sufficient powers or resources to help the city.

The principle of discrimination between areas with different problems and needs is well established. If it could be developed to include broader urban development strategies, the long term needs of Liverpool, as well as other cities, might be more sensibly addressed. Such strategies might resemble the current urban programme system. They would include a standard grant determined by the size of population, combined with capital and revenue budgets for housing, transport, education, health and economic development, varied according to the different longer term plan developed for each city. They would also give Government a more positive role in making policy for the cities, as opposed to the powerful, but restraining, role it currently has.

Recent experience shows it is difficult to make these kinds of initiatives work. However, the important thing is that, like in many other countries, they would make the relationship between the Government and the cities less an administrative one and more directly political.

And the Minister for Merseyside would have real authority to commit the resources of his own and other Government Departments. This would place a premium upon the capacity of both sides to bargain and negotiate. There could be political benefits in that relationship. If the Government did not act fairly or local leaders were not smart enough to get a good deal for their city, people would know, more clearly than they do in Liverpool today, who to blame.